80486 System Architecture

Third Edition

MINDSHARE, INC.

TOM SHANLEY

Addison-Wesley Publishing Company
Reading, Massachusetts • Menlo Park, California • New York
Don Mills, Ontario • Wokingham, England • Amsterdam
Bonn • Sydney • Singapore • Tokyo • Madrid • San Juan
Paris • Seoul • Milan • Mexico City • Taipei

Library of Congress Cataloging-in-Publication Data

ISBN: 0-201-40994-1

Sponsoring Editor: Keith Wollman
Project Manager: Eleanor McCarthy
Production Coordinator: Deborah McKenna
Cover design: Barbara T. Atkinson
Set in 10 point Palatino by MindShare, Inc.

1 2 3 4 5 6 7 8 9 -MA- 9998979695
First printing, April 1995

Addison-Wesley books are available for bulk purchases by corporations, institutions, and other organizations. For more information please contact the Corporate, Government, and Special Sales Department at (800) 238-9682.

For the best and brightest: my mother and father.

This book would not have been possible without the input of hundreds of hardware and software people at Compaq, IBM, Intel, and Dell over the past several years. They constantly sanity-check me and make me tell the truth.

Special thanks to Don Anderson, the best hiking partner and an even better teacher.

Contents

About This Book

Chapter 1: 80486 Overview

Chapter 2: Functional Units

Chapter 3: The Hardware Interface

Chapter 4: The 486 Cache and Line Fill Operations

Contents

Chapter 5: Bus Transactions (Non-Cache)

Chapter 6: SL Technology

Chapter 7: Summary of Software Changes

Chapter 8: The 486SX and 487SX Processors

Chapter 9: The 486DX2 and 486SX2 Processors

Chapter 10: The Write Back Enhanced 486DX2

Chapter 11: The 486DX4 Processor

Figures

Tables

The MindShare Architecture Series

The series of books by MindShare on system architecture includes; *ISA System Architecture, EISA System Architecture, 80486 System Architecture, PCI System Architecture, Pentium™ Processor System Architecture, PCMCIA System Architecture, PowerPC™ System Architecture, Plug and Play System Architecture,* and *AMD K5 System Architecture,* all published by Addison-Wesley.

Rather than duplicating common information in each book, the series uses a building-block approach. *ISA System Architecture* is the core book upon which the others build. The figure below illustrates the relationship of the books to each other.

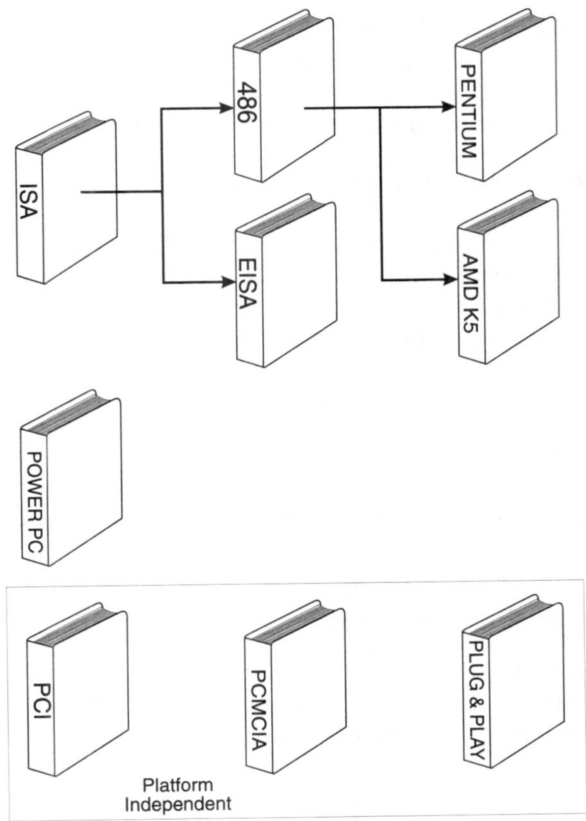

Architecture Series Organization

Organization of This Book

80486 System Architecture consists of eleven chapters and the appendices. Chapter 1 introduces the entire family of Intel 486 processors. Chapters 2 through 7 cover the core technology that is common to the entire 486 product line, with a few exceptions. For example, chapter 4 discusses the internal cache structure which is common to all 486 processors except for the Write Back Enhanced 486DX2 and the 486DX4 processors. Respective chapters on these processors detail the differences. In this manner, chapters 8 through 11 discuss the differences between the standard 486DX and other processors in the 486 family. The following provides a brief discription of the contents of each chapter.

Chapter 1: 80486 Overview — This chapter introduces the performance bottlenecks that existed in all x86 processors prior to the introduction of the 80486 and defines the solutions implemented by the 486 to alleviate these performance problems. The 80486 microarchitecture is also introduced along with the other 80486 processors that comprise the Intel 486 processor family.

Chapter 2: Functional Units — This chapter discusses the major functional units within the i486DX microprocessor. The functional units consist of the Bus Interface Unit, Cache Unit, Instruction Pipeline/Decode Unit (consisting of the Instruction Prefetcher and Instruction Decode Units), Control Unit, Floating-Point Unit, Data Path Unit (integer execution), Memory Management Unit (consisting of the paging and segment units).

Chapter 3: The Hardware Interface — This chapter defines each of the 486DX processor's external pins and describes their functions. Later chapters detail signals that are specific to a particular version of processor.

Chapter 4: The 486 Cache and Line Fill Operations — This chapter details the operation of the internal data cache including cache-related bus cycles that can be run by the 486 processors. The interaction between the 486 internal cache and L2 cache are also discussed.

Chapter 5: Bus Transactions (Non-Cache) — This chapter summarizes and defines the bus transactions that can be run by the 80486 microprocessor, with emphasis on non-cache transactions.

Chapter 6: SL Technology — This chapter discusses the SL Technology features implemented in the 486DX family of processors. Focus is placed on System Management Mode (SMM) and clock control.

Chapter 7: Summary of Software Changes — This chapter discusses the changes to the x86 software environment introduced and implemented in the latest 486DX processors.

Chapter 8: The 486SX and 487SX Processors — This chapter details the differences between the 486SX processors and the 486DX processors.

Chapter 9: The 486DX2 and 486SX2 Processors — This chapter introduces the 486DX2 and 486SX2 processors and highlights the differences between them and the 486DX and SX processors.

Chapter 10: Write Back Enhanced 486DX2 Processor — This chapter discusses the features associated with the Enhanced Write Back 486DX2 and the differences between it and the standard 486DX2 processors. The chapter focuses on new signals, the MESI model, special cycles, and cache line fill and snoop transactions.

Chapter 11: The 486DX4 Processor — This chapter overviews the 486DX4 processor and discusses the differences between the it and other 486 processors.

Appendices — The appendices are segmented into four sections and are intended for quick reference. The appendices include:

- Glossary of Terms
- References

Who Should Read This Book

This book is intended for use by hardware and software design and support personnel. Due to the clear, concise explanatory methods used to describe each subject, personnel outside of the design field may also find the text useful.

Prerequisite Knowledge

We highly recommend that you have a good knowledge of the PC architecture prior to reading this book. The publications entitled *ISA System Architecture* provides all of the background necessary for a complete understanding of the subject matter covered in this book. Also the chapter entitled "Summary of Software Changes," assumes knowledge of the 80386 registers and software environment. See the publication entitled *ISA System Architecture* for background information on the software environment.

Documentation Conventions

This section defines the typographical conventions used throughout this book.

Hex Notation

All hex numbers are followed by an "h." Examples:

9A4Eh
0100h

Binary Notation

All binary numbers are followed by a "b." Examples:

0001 0101b
01b

Decimal Notation

When required for clarity, decimal numbers are followed by a "d." Examples:

256d
128d

Signal Name Representation

Each signal that assumes the logic low state when asserted is followed by a pound sign (#). As an example, the BRDY# signal is asserted low when a target device is ready to complete a data transfer.

Signals that are not followed by a pound sign are asserted when they assume the logic high state. As an example, BREQ is asserted high to indicate that the 486 processor needs control of the buses to perform a bus operation.

Identification of Bit Fields

All bit fields are designated as follows:

X:Y,

where "X" is the most-significant bit and "Y" is the least-significant bit of the field. As an example, the 80486 address bus consists of A31:A2, where A31 is the most-significant and A2 the least-significant bit of the field.

We Want Your Feedback

MindShare values your comments and suggestions. You can contact us via mail, phone, fax, BBS or internet email.

E-Mail/Phone/FAX

Email: mindshar@interserv.com
Phone: (214) 231-2216
Fax: (214) 783-4715

Bulletin Board

BBS: (214) 705-9604

Because we are constantly on the road teaching, we can be difficult to contact. To help alleviate problems associated with our migratory habits, we have initiated a bulletin board to supply the following services:

- Download course abstracts.
- Automatic registration for public seminars.
- Message area to make inquiries about public seminars.
- Message area to log technical questions.
- Message area to log comments on MindShare books and seminars.

Mailing Address

Our mailing address is:

MindShare, Inc.
2202 Buttercup Drive
Richardson, Texas 75082

Chapter 1

This Chapter

This chapter introduces the performance bottlenecks that existed in all x86 processors prior to the introduction of the 80486 and defines the solutions implemented by the 486 to alleviate these performance problems. The 80486 microarchitecture is also introduced along with the other 80486 processors that comprise the Intel 486 processor family.

The Next Chapter

The next chapter defines and discusses the major functional units within the i486DX microprocessor.

System Performance Prior to the 80486

Systems based on x86 processors prior to the introduction of the 80486 microprocessor were hampered by the relatively slow access to memory and by a rather cumbersome floating-point unit interface. The 80486 design significantly reduces the effects of these problems. The following sections explore these performance bottlenecks and introduces the 80486 solutions.

The Memory Bottleneck

When 80386 microprocessor speeds reached the 20 to 25MHz vicinity, reasonably-priced DRAM memory could no longer be accessed with zero wait state bus cycles. One or more wait states would be inserted into every bus cycle that accessed memory. Memory access time, therefore, became a serious impediment to good processor and system performance. There were two possible solutions:

- Populate the entire memory with SRAMs
- Implement a cache subsystem

The Static Ram, or SRAM, Solution

In order to gain the maximum performance benefit of the faster and more powerful processors, faster and more expensive static RAM, or SRAM, devices must be used. SRAM is easily capable of providing zero wait state performance at higher processor speeds; however, for several reasons, this solution is not economically viable:

- SRAM is typically ten times more expensive than DRAM memory.
- SRAM chips are physically larger than DRAMs, requiring more real-estate for the same amount of memory.
- SRAMs consume more power than DRAMs and may require a more powerful, and therefore more expensive, power supply.
- SRAMs generate more heat than DRAMs and may therefore require a larger cooling fan.

The External Cache Solution

Advantage: Reduces Many Memory Accesses to Zero Wait States

System designers achieved a performance/cost trade off by implementing an external cache consisting of a relatively small amount of SRAM coupled with a cache controller, and populating the bulk of system memory with inexpensive DRAM memory. The cache controller attempts to keep copies of frequently requested information in SRAM so that it can be accessed quickly if requested again. If the controller experiences a high percentage of hits on the cache, the number of memory accesses requiring the insertion of wait states is substantially reduced.

Disadvantage: Memory Accesses Still Bound By Bus Speed

A drawback associated with the external cache approach (when the processor does not incorporate an internal cache) is that every memory request requires a bus cycle and even zero wait state bus cycles take time. The bus speed presents a bottleneck to processor performance.

The 80486 Solution: Internal Code/Data Cache

As pointed out in the previous section, an external cache provides important performance improvements, but the processor must still perform memory read bus cycles to fetch data and code.

Faster Memory Accesses

The 486 alleviates this problem by moving the cache on board the processor chip itself. When the requested code or data is found in the internal cache, memory read requests initiated by the processor core can then be fulfilled from the cache without running bus cycles. The only delay incurred is that necessary to perform the internal cache lookup and to deliver the target data or code to the internal requester. Due to the exceedingly short length of the data paths involved and the fast access time of the on-board SRAM these accesses will complete appreciably faster than would zero wait state bus cycles.

Frees Up the Bus

Every time a memory read request is fulfilled from the on-chip cache one less bus cycle needs to be run on the external buses. This frees up the buses for use by other bus masters in the system. The processor core can be feeding out of its internal cache at the same time that another bus master is using the external buses to perform a data transfer. The bus concurrency thus achieved improves the overall performance of the system.

The Floating-Point Bottleneck

Prior to the 80486 microprocessor the x86 processors had a companion processor that performed floating-point operations. These numeric coprocessors required transactions between the main processor and the coprocessor. Each x86 processor/coprocessor pair had a slightly different interface. The following section describes interaction between the 80386 processor and 80387 coprocessor and highlights the performance bottleneck that exist.

The 80386/80387 Solution

The microprocessor treats the 80387 numeric coprocessor as an I/O device. When the 80386 microprocessor fetches and detects a floating-point instruction from memory, it must pass the instruction to the 80387 for execution. Upon detecting the floating-point instruction the 80386 automatically performs a series of one or more I/O writes to forward the instruction to the coprocessor. Since a series of bus cycle are needed to pass the instruction to the 80387, this adds considerable overhead when executing floating-point instructions.

Furthermore, if the floating point instruction requires that a floating-point operand be fetched from memory or written to memory, the processor is once again required to perform the bus cycles needed to move data. The 80386 must partially decode each floating point instruction to determine if it will be required to perform bus cycles specified by the floating-point instruction. The 80386 stores the memory address location along with the transfer type (read or write) and performs the bus cycle when requested by the 80387. Two bus cycles are required: one to read the data (from memory or an 80387 register) and one to write data (to memory or an 80387 register).

The 80486 Solution: Integrate the FPU

The 80486 has the floating-point unit (FPU) integrated into the processor. This eliminates the additional bus cycles needed to pass instructions and data between the processor and the external numeric coprocessor. Furthermore, since the 80486 contains an internal cache, a floating-point instruction can be fetched, data operands can be read, the instruction executed, and data operands written back to memory without a single bus cycle being performed.

The 80486 Microarchitecture

The Intel 80486 microprocessor can be viewed as an enhanced 80386 with memory cache and floating-point unit incorporated on the same silicon substrate. Refer to figure 1-1.

Due to the high level of integration, the system designer can implement very powerful systems with a relatively low chip count. In addition, some aspects of the microprocessor's design have been streamlined to allow simplification of system design.

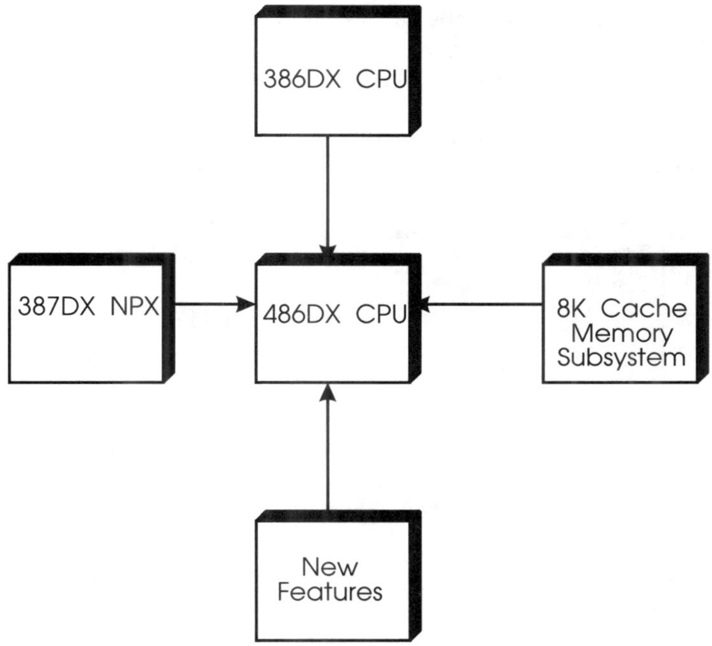

Figure 1-1. Subsystems Integrated into the 80486

As illustrated in figure 1-1, the 80486 microprocessor consists of a number of system elements incorporated on one chip:

- enhanced 80386 microprocessor
- 80387 Floating-Point Processor
- cache memory controller and 8KB of cache memory
- additional new features

From a software perspective, the 80486 is a superset of the 80386. The changes include:

- new instructions
- new bits in existent registers
- deleted bits in existent registers
- new registers added
- new bits defined in page directory and page table entries

The Intel Family of 486 Processors

Since Intel introduced the first i486DX processor many variations of the original processor have been introduced. Table 1-1 lists the different 486 processors and describes their main features.

Table 1-1. Intel's 486 Family of Processors

Processor	Vcc	Core Frequency	Key Features
i486DX	5.0v 3.3v	33; 50 33	• 8KB unified internal cache • Write-through policy • Integrated floating-point unit • Burst bus cycle support • System Management Mode (SMM)*
i486SX	3.3 & 5v	25; 33	Same as i486DX except: No floating-point unit
i486SX2	5v	50	Same as i486SX except: Clock doubler with a bus to processor core frequency ration of 1 to 2. 25MHz bus & 50MHz core
i486DX2	5v 3.3v	50; 66 40; 50	Same as i486DX except: Clock doubler with a bus to processor core frequency ration of 1 to 2. 20MHz bus & 40MHz core 25MHz bus & 50MHz core 33MHz bus & 66MHz core
i486DX2 (enh. write)	5v 3.3v	50; 66 40; 50	Same as i486DX except: Write-back cache policy
i486DX4	3.3v	75; 83; 100	Same as i486DX except: • 16KB unified internal cache • Clock multiplier with selectable bus to core processor ratio (1/2, 1/2.5, or 1/3). 25MHz bus & 75MHz core 33MHz bus & 83MHz core 33MHz bus & 100MHz core 50MHz bus & 100MHz core

* All Intel 486 processors now have SMM capability, however the initial i486DX and i486DX processors did not incorporate SMM. These earlier models have been discontinued.

Chapter 2

The Previous Chapter

The previous chapter introduced the performance bottlenecks that existed in all x86 processors prior to the introduction of the 80486 and defined the solutions implemented by the 80486 microprocessor to alleviate these performance problems. The 80486 microarchitecture was also introduced along with the other 80486 processors that comprise the Intel 486 processor family.

This Chapter

This chapter discusses the major functional units within the i486DX microprocessor.

The Next Chapter

The next chapter defines each of the 486DX processor external pins and describes their functions.

The 80486 Functional Units

Introduction

The 80486 microprocessor consists of the functional units illustrated in figure 2-1:

- Bus Interface Unit
- Cache Unit
- Instruction Pipeline/Decode Unit (consists of instruction prefetch and instruction decode units)
- Control Unit
- Floating-Point Unit

- Data Path Unit
- Memory Management Unit (MMU consists of paging and segment units)

The following sections describe each of these functional units.

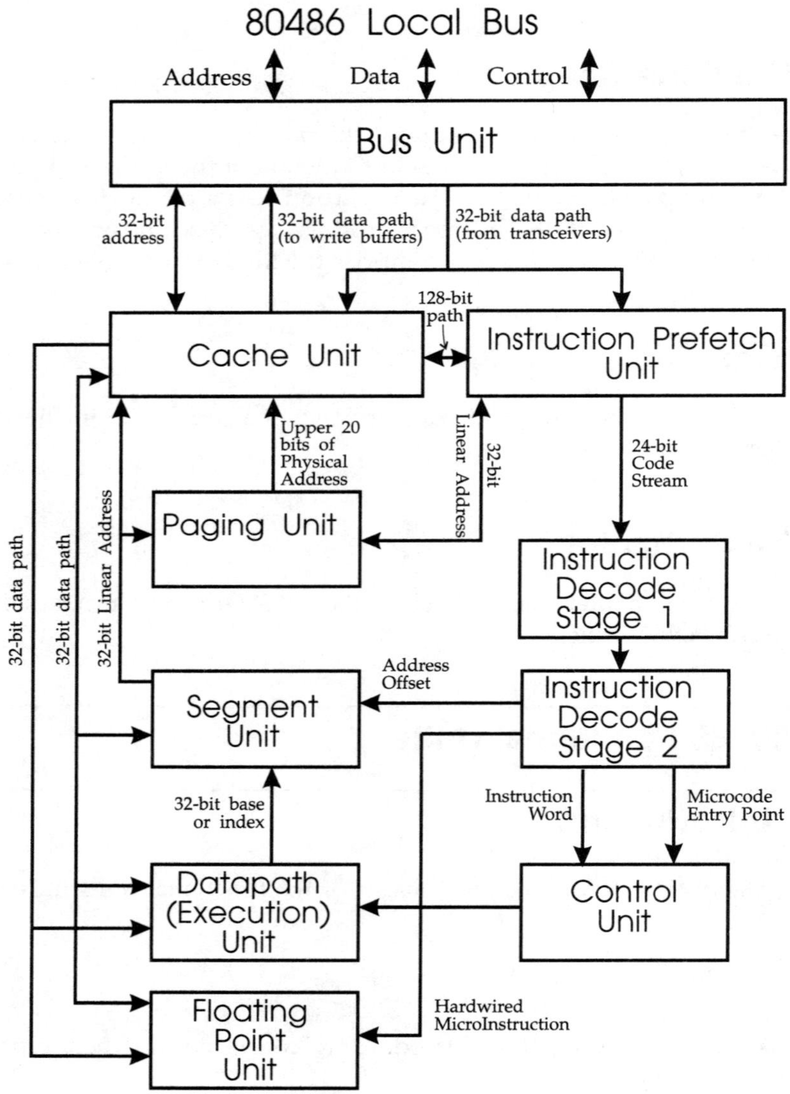

Figure 2-1. 80486 Microarchitecture

The 80486 Bus Unit

The bus unit provides the physical interface between the 80486 and external devices. Refer to figure 2-2. The bus unit consists of the following functional entities:

- Address drivers/receivers. When the 80486 is executing a bus cycle, the address drivers are used to drive the address out onto the processor's local address bus (A31:A2) and the byte enable lines. During cache invalidation cycles, address bits A31:A4 are input from the processor's local address bus through the address receivers.
- Write buffers. These four buffers allow the bus unit to buffer up to four write bus cycles from the processor, permitting these write operations to complete execution instantly.
- Data bus transceivers. Used to gate data onto the processor's local data bus during write bus cycles. Used to gate data into the processor from the processor's local data bus during read bus cycles.
- Bus size control logic. Senses when the microprocessor is communicating with 8- or 16-bit devices, causing the microprocessor to automatically execute multiple bus cycles when necessary.
- Bus control request sequencer. Determines the order of addressing during burst transfers.
- Burst bus control logic. Used to control the buses during the execution of a burst transfer.
- Cache control logic. Connects the processor's local buses to the external cache controller.
- Parity generation/checking logic. Automatically generates even parity on data being written by the microprocessor and checks for valid even parity during read bus cycles.

The 80486 Cache Unit

The 80486 microprocessor incorporates a cache controller and 8KB of fast access static RAM cache memory. The directory structure used by the cache controller is four-way set associative. An in-depth description of the on-chip cache can be found later in this document.

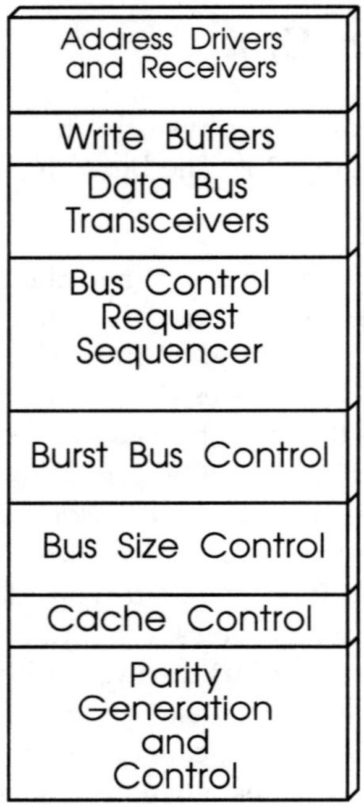

Figure 2-2. The Elements Comprising the 80486 Bus Unit

The Instruction Pipeline/Decode Unit

The instruction pipeline/decode unit consists of three basic parts:

- Prefetcher
- 32 byte code queue
- Instruction decoder

The 80486 microprocessor incorporates a five-deep pipeline that significantly speeds up instruction decode and execution:

- Instruction prefetch
- Stage 1 decode
- Stage 2 decode
- Execution
- Register write-back

At a given moment in time, a series of instructions are in the pipeline at various stages. The ability of the 80486 microprocessor to process a number of instructions in parallel in this fashion gives it the ability to complete execution of an instruction during each cycle of the processor clock (PCLK). However, this capability depends on the particular instructions in the instruction stream. Refer to figure 2-3.

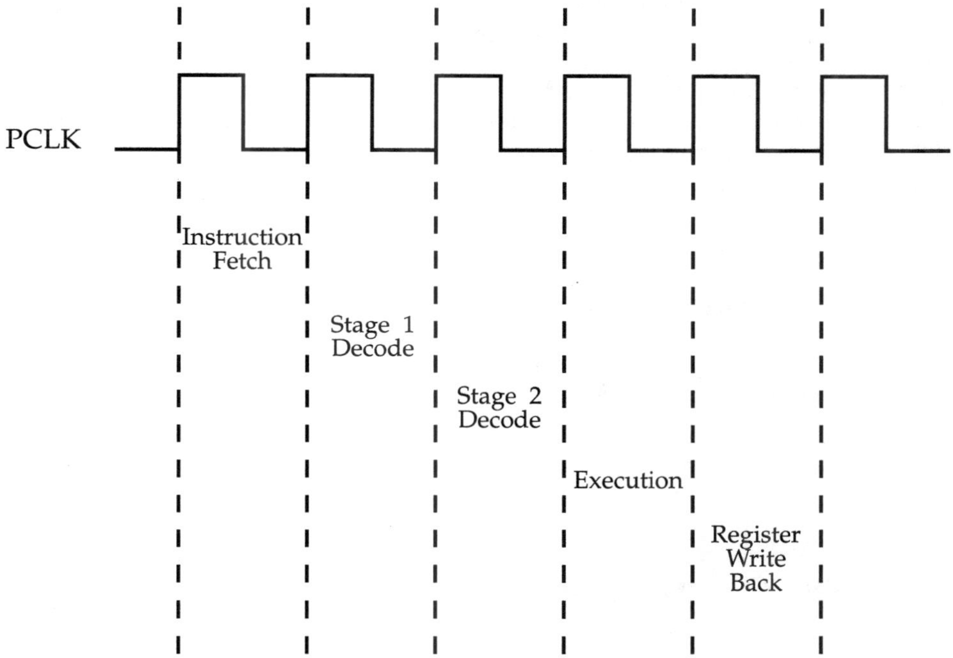

Figure 2-3. 80486 Instruction Pipeline

Instruction Prefetch

The Prefetcher reads instructions in 16-byte blocks (lines). The line of code is read into both the internal cache and the 32-byte prefetch queue.

Two-Stage Instruction Decode

During the stage 1 decode, the opcode byte is decoded, the optional MOD R/M byte is interpreted to indicate the form of addressing to be used and the optional Scale Index Byte (SIB) is used to more fully specify the form of addressing. If this terminology doesn't mean anything to you, it's because you aren't an assembly language programmer. An explanation of these terms can be found in the Intel programmer's reference manual.

During the stage 2 decode, the displacement is added to the address and any immediate operands are taken into account. Once again, these terms are only meaningful to assembly language programmers.

Execution

The instruction is executed.

Register Write-Back

Instruction execution is completed and the result written back to a target register (if necessary).

The Control Unit

Also referred to as the microcode unit, the control unit consists of the following sub-units:

- the microcode sequencer
- the microcode control ROM

This unit interprets the instruction word and microcode entry points fed to it by the instruction decode unit. It handles exceptions, breakpoints and interrupts. In addition, it controls integer and floating-point sequences.

The Floating-Point Unit

The floating-point unit executes the same instruction set as the 80387 Numeric Co-Processor extension. It shares microcode ROM, instruction decode and address pipelining logic with the datapath, or integer execution, unit. The floating-point unit consists of two tightly-coupled sub-units:

- the floating-point unit
- the floating-point register file. Contains the registers indigenous to the floating-point unit.

The Numeric Exception (NE) control bit in CR0 allows the programmer to select the error handling scenario to be used by the microprocessor when a floating-point error is detected. Setting this bit to 1 causes the microprocessor to generate an internal exception 16 interrupt when the floating-point unit incurs an error.

If the programmer wishes the processor to use the PC-DOS-compatible error reporting technique for floating-point errors, this bit should be set to 0. PC-DOS uses interrupt request level 13 to report this type of error.

In either case, a floating-point error causes the microprocessor's FERR# output to be asserted. This pin is the equivalent of the 287/387 ERROR output. Refer to the chapter entitled "Summary of Software Changes" for details related to floating-point error handling.

The Datapath Unit

The datapath unit contains the following sub-units:

- General-purpose registers. These registers are discussed in detail in the chapter entitled, "A Summary of Software Changes."
- Arithmetic logic unit (ALU). This unit handles all integer and bit-oriented math functions.
- Barrel shifter. Used by the ALU to perform math functions.
- Flags. The flag register basically consists of two bit fields:
- The flag status bits reflect the results of the previously executed instruction.

- The flag control bits allow the programmer to alter certain operational characteristics of the microprocessor.

The datapath unit also contains special stack pointer logic to accommodate single-clock pushes and pops. In addition, single load, store, add, subtract, logic and shift instructions can be executed in one clock.

The Memory Management Unit (MMU)

The MMU consists of two sub-units:

- The segmentation unit. Calculates effective (paging unit off) and linear (paging unit on) addresses from the segment and offset. It has been redesigned to generate one address per clock. The segmentation unit contains the segment descriptor cache. It also performs limit and access rights checks.
- The paging unit. If enabled by setting the PG bit in CR0, the paging unit translates the linear address to a physical address. It performs the same functions as the 80386 microprocessor's paging mechanism, but has been optimized to improve system performance. It can perform one translation look-aside buffer (TLB) lookup per clock. Individual pages may now be write-protected against supervisor access.

Chapter 3

The Previous Chapter

The previous chapter discussed the major functional units within the i486DX microprocessor.

This Chapter

This chapter defines each of the 486DX processor's external pins and describes their functions.

The Next Chapter

The next chapter details the operation of the internal data cache including cache-related bus cycles that can be run by the i486DX processor. The interaction between the 486 internal cache and external caches are also discussed.

Hardware Interface

General

Figure 3-1 illustrates the signal interface for the 80486DX and 80486SX processors. Tables 3-1 through 3-19 define the pinouts which have been logically grouped according to function.

Note also that the boundary scan interface shown in figure 3-1 was initially available only on the 486DX 50MHz processor, but has now been added to all 486DX processors.

Today's 486DX processors also include the SL technology interface that supports System Management Mode (SMM) and stop clock (STPCLK#). This functionality was not present in earlier 486DX versions. The 50MHz 486DX is the only current 486 processor that does not support the SL technology features.

The floating-point unit (FPU) is not integrated into the 486SX processors, therefore the floating-point error reporting signals (FERR# and IGNNE#) are not defined for the 486SX processors.

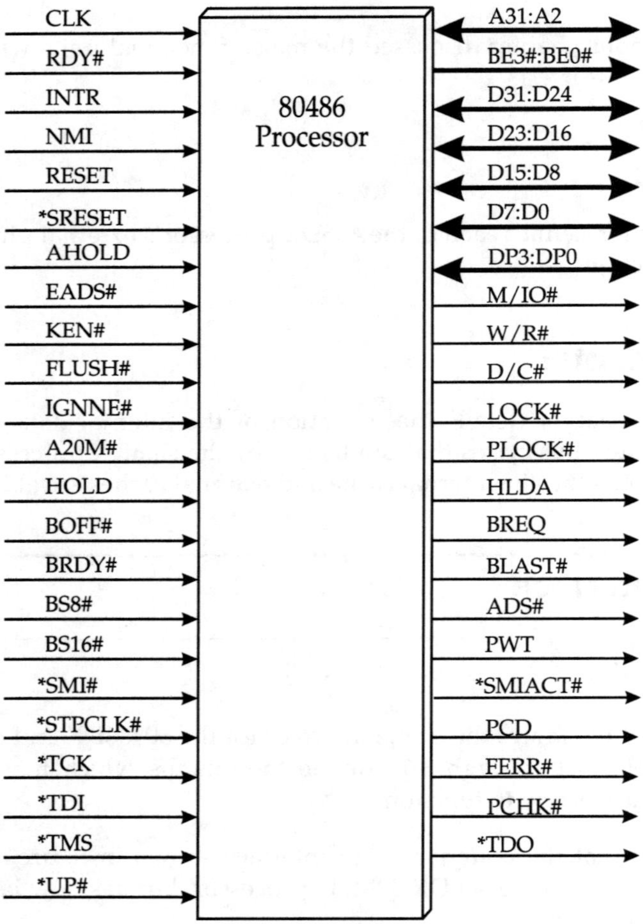

Figure 3-1. 80486 Pin Designations

* These pins were not implemented on the original 486DX processors. Note however, that the boundary scan interface was implemented on the original 50MHz 486DX.

Clock

Table 3-1. Clock-Related Signals

Signal	I/O	Description
CLK	I	**Clock** provides the fundamental timing and the internal operating frequency for the 80486 microprocessor. Unlike the double-frequency clock necessary for proper operation of previous Intel microprocessors, this clock is not divided by two inside the microprocessor. This was done to simplify system design and minimize the problems inherent in the design of high frequency systems.

Address

Table 3-2. Address-Related Signals

Signal	I/O	Description
BE0#	O	The **byte enable** is asserted by the microprocessor to indicate that the 80486 wishes to perform a transfer between itself and the first location (byte 0) in the currently addressed doubleword over the first data path, D7:D0.
BE1#	O	Asserted by the microprocessor to indicate that the 80486 wishes to perform a transfer between itself and the second location (byte 1) in the currently addressed doubleword over the second data path, D15:D8.
BE2#	O	Asserted by the microprocessor to indicate that the 80486 wishes to perform a transfer between itself and the third location (byte 2) in the currently addressed doubleword over the third data path, D23:D16.
BE3#	O	Asserted by the microprocessor to indicate that the 80486 wishes to perform a transfer between itself and the fourth location (byte 3) in the currently addressed doubleword over the fourth data path, D31:D24.

Table 3-2, continued

Signal	I/O	Description
A31:A2	I/O	A31:A2 comprise the 80486 microprocessor's address bus. When the 80486 wishes to address an external device, the address is driven out onto the address bus. Address bits 0 and 1 do not exist and should always be treated as if zero. This means that the 80486 is only capable of placing the address of every fourth location on the address bus (0, 4, 8, C, 10, etc.). This is known as the doubleword address , and identifies a group of four locations starting at the indicated address. This group of four locations is known as a doubleword. The microprocessor uses the four Byte Enable outputs, BE0#:BE3#, to indicate which of the four locations in the doubleword it wishes to communicate with and to also indicate the data path to be used when communicating with each location in the doubleword. A3:A2 are output-only, while A31:A4 are bidirectional. A31:A4 are used to drive line addresses into the microprocessor during cache line invalidations (bus snooping).

Data Bus

Table 3-3. Data Bus

Signal	I/O	Description
D7:D0	I/O	This data path (path 0) is used to transfer data between the 80486 and the first location (byte 0) in the currently addressed doubleword. See also A31:A2 and BE0#.
D15:D8	I/O	This data path (path 1) is used to transfer data between the 80486 and the second location (byte 1) in the currently addressed doubleword. See also A31:A2 and BE1#.
D23:D16	I/O	This data path (path 2) is used to transfer data between the 80486 and the third location (byte 2) in the currently addressed doubleword. See also A31:A2 and BE2#.
D31:D24	I/O	This data path (path 3) is used to transfer data between the 80486 and the fourth location (byte 3) in the currently addressed doubleword. See also A31:A2 and BE3#.

Data Bus Parity

Table 3-4. The Data Bus Parity Signals

Signal	I/O	Description
DP0	I/O	This is the **parity bit for data path 0**, D7:D0. Even data parity is generated on all write bus cycles and is checked on all read bus cycles. If a parity error is detected on a read operation, the 80486 is not affected, but will assert its PCHK# output. The parity error can then be handled by external logic.
DP1	I/O	This is the **parity bit for data path 1**, D15:D8. See explanation of DP0.
DP2	I/O	This is the **parity bit for data path 2**, D23:D16. See explanation of DP0.
DP3	I/O	This is the **parity bit for data path 3**, D31:D24. See explanation of DP0.
PCHK#	O	**Data Parity Check**. See explanation for DP0.

Bus Cycle Definition

Table 3-5 describes the 80486 outputs used to define the type of bus cycle in progress.

Table 3-5. Bus Cycle Definition Signals

Signal	I/O	Description
LOCK#	O	**LOCK#** is automatically generated by the 80486 when it is executing an instruction that performs a memory read immediately followed by a memory write. This includes updates to segment descriptor, page directory and page table entries, and execution of the XCHG instruction when one of the operands is memory-based. The processor also automatically asserts LOCK# during the two back-to-back Interrupt Acknowledge bus cycles issued in response to an interrupt request. In addition, the processor will assert LOCK# when executing instructions prefaced by the LOCK prefix. When active, the bus lock pin indicates that the current bus cycle is locked. The 80486 microprocessor will not allow a Bus Hold from an external bus master when LOCK# is asserted (Address Holds, caused by the assertion of AHOLD, are allowed, however). LOCK# goes active in the first clock of the first locked bus cycle and goes inactive after the last clock of the last locked bus cycle. The last locked bus cycle ends when ready is returned.
PLOCK#	O	The processor automatically asserts **Pseudo-Lock** when reading or writing an operand that requires multiple bus cycles to complete. Examples of such operations are floating-point long reads and writes (8-byte transfer), segment table descriptor reads (8-byte transfer), as well as cache line fills (16-byte transfer). The 80486 will drive PLOCK# active until the address for the last bus cycle of the transaction has been driven onto the address bus regardless of whether RDY# or BRDY# have been returned.
M/IO#	O	**Memory or I/O#**. At the start of a bus cycle, the 80486 sets this line high if addressing a memory location and low if addressing an I/O location. Combined with D/C# and W/R#, comprises the 80486's Bus Cycle Definition lines.

Table 3-5, continued

Signal	I/O	Description
D/C#	O	**Data or Control#**. At the start of a bus cycle, the 80486 sets this line high if data (not code) will be transferred during the current bus cycle. It sets D/C# low if the current bus cycle is not a data transfer bus cycle (Interrupt Acknowledge, Halt/Special or a code read bus cycle).
W/R#	O	**Write or Read#**. At the start of a bus cycle, the 80486 sets this line high if the current bus cycle is a write bus cycle (memory or I/O). W/R# is set low if the current bus cycle is a read bus cycle (memory or I/O).

Bus Cycle Control

Table 3-6. Bus Cycle Control Signals

Signal	I/O	Description
ADS	O	When active, the **Address Status** output indicates that a valid bus cycle definition and address are available on the Bus Cycle Definition and address bus lines.
RDY#	I	The **non-burst Ready** input indicates that the current bus cycle is complete. RDY indicates that the currently addressed device has presented valid data on the data bus pins in response to a read or that the currently addressed device has accepted data from the 80486 in response to a write.

Burst Control

Table 3-7. Burst Control Signals

Signal	I/O	Description
BRDY#	I	The **Burst Ready** input performs the same function during a burst cycle that RDY# performs during a non-burst cycle. BRDY# indicates that the currently addressed device has presented valid data on the data bus pins in response to a read or that the currently addressed device has accepted data from the 80486 in response to a write. BRDY# is sampled in the second and subsequent clocks of a burst cycle. The data presented on the data bus will be strobed into the microprocessor when BRDY# is sampled active. If RDY# is presented simultaneously with BRDY#, BRDY# is ignored and the burst cycle is prematurely terminated.
BLAST#	O	The **Burst Last** signal indicates that the next time BRDY# is returned, the burst cycle is complete. The 486 processor deasserts BLAST# to notify external logic that it is willing to perform a burst bus cycle. If RDY#, rather than BRDY# is returned to the processor the bus cycle ends without a burst cycle.

Interrupts

Several input pins to the 486 processor are recognized as interrupt inputs in addition to INTR and NMI listed in table 3-8. The other 486 pins that are implemented as interrupts include:

- RESET (refer to page 34)
- SRESET (refer to page 34)
- SMI# (refer to page 33)

Table 3-8. Interrupt-Related Signals

Signal	I/O	Description
INTR	I	This is the **maskable Interrupt Request** input. If interrupt recognition is enabled when INTR is asserted, the 80486 will service the interrupt request.

Table 3-8, continued

Signal	I/O	Description
NMI	I	When sensed active, the **Non-Maskable Interrupt Request** signal causes the 80486 to immediately suspend normal program execution and begin to service the NMI. After saving the CS, EIP and EFlag register contents on the stack, the 80486 will jump to the NMI Interrupt Service Routine through Interrupt Table slot 2.

Bus Arbitration

Table 3-9. Bus Arbitration-Related Signals

Signal	I/O	Description
BREQ	O	The **Bus Cycle Request** signal indicates that an internal bus cycle is request is pending inside the 80486 microprocessor. BREQ is generated whether or not the 80486 microprocessor is currently the bus master. It is used by a CPU bus arbitrator in a multiple-processor system to determine which processors are currently requesting the host bus.
HOLD	I	The **Bus Hold Request** input allows another bus master to gain complete control of the 80486's local buses. In response to HOLD going active, the 80486 will disconnect itself from most of its output pins after the current bus cycle completes. HLDA (Hold Acknowledge) is then asserted to inform the requesting bus master that is now the owner of the external bus structure and can run a bus cycle. The 80486 microprocessor will not be able to use the external buses again until the current bus master de-asserts HOLD.
HLDA	O	**Bus Hold Acknowledge**. See the description of HOLD above.
BOFF#	I	Backoff is used to ensure that the processor doesn't fetch stale data from main memory. The Backoff input forces the 80486 microprocessor to float its buses in the next clock. The microprocessor will disconnect itself from its external buses, but will not assert HLDA. BOFF# has a higher priority than RDY# or BRDY#. If a bus cycle was in progress when BOFF# was asserted, the bus cycle will be restarted when BOFF# is de-asserted.

Cache Invalidation

Table 3-10. Cache Invalidation-Related Signals

Signal	I/O	Description
AHOLD	I	The **Address Hold Request** input allows another bus master access to the 80486 microprocessor's address bus for a cache invalidation cycle. This is necessary if a bus master other than the 80486 is altering a main memory location that may be cached in the 80486's internal cache. In response to the assertion of AHOLD, the 80486 will stop driving its address bus in the clock following AHOLD going active. Only the address bus will be floated during Address Hold. The remainder of the buses will remain active. See also EADS# below.
EADS#	I	The **External Address Strobe** signal indicates that a valid external address has been driven onto the 80486's A31:A4 address lines by another bus master. This address will be used to perform an internal cache invalidation cycle (snoop). As a result, if a cache directory entry indicates that a cache line has a copy of the addressed memory data (snoop hit), the directory entry will be marked to show that the line is no longer valid. Also see the description of AHOLD.

Cache Control

Table 3-11. Internal Cache Control-Related Signals

Signal	I/O	Description
KEN#	I	The **Cache Enable** pin is sampled to determine if the current bus cycle is cacheable (from memory's point of view). When the 80486 generates a memory read bus cycle that the processor would like to cache and KEN# is sampled active, the bus cycle will be converted to a cache fill cycle. Returning KEN# active one clock before the last ready during the last read in the cache line fill will cause the line to be placed in the on-chip cache.
FLUSH#	I	The **Cache Flush** input forces the 80486 to flush the contents of its internal cache.

Table 3-12. L2 Cache-Related Signals

<table>
<tr><th>Signal</th><th>I/O</th><th>Description</th></tr>
<tr><td>PCD</td><td>O</td><td>The Page Cache Disable pin, when asserted, notifies the L2 cache (if implemented) that the memory transaction currently being performed is not cacheable. The state of PCD depends on whether paging is enabled and the type of bus cycle being performed.

When paging is disabled and any time the processor performs a non-memory transactions, the processor deasserts PCD.

When paging is enabled the state of PCD depends on the state of the PCD bit. The source of the PCD bit depends on the memory transaction being performed as follows:
• The PCD bit in CR3 determines the state of the PCD pin when the processor accesses the page directory from memory.
• The PCD bit in the page directory entry determines the state of the PCD pin when the processor accesses a page table from memory.
• The PCD bit in the page table entry determines the state of the PCD pin when the processor accesses a 4KB page from memory.
Note that the PCD bit in CR0 gates the PCD pin, thereby providing a method of forcing the PCD pin to zero (deasserted) even when paging is enabled.</td></tr>
<tr><td>PWT</td><td>O</td><td>The Page Write Through pin, when asserted, notifies a write-back L2 cache controller (if implemented) that the memory write transaction currently being performed should be written through the main memory (not treated as a write-back operation). The state of PWT depends on whether paging is enabled and the type of bus cycle being performed.

When paging is disabled and any time the processor performs a transaction other than a memory transfer, the processor deasserts PWT.

When paging is enabled the state of PWT depends on the state of the appropriate PWT bit. The source of the PWT bit depends on the memory transaction being performed as follows:
• The PWT bit within CR3 determines the state of the PWT pin when the processor accesses the page directory from memory.
• The PWT bit within the page directory entry determines the state of the PWT pin when the processor accesses a page table from memory.

The PWT bit within the page table entry determines the state of the PWT pin when the processor accesses a 4KB page from memory.</td></tr>
</table>

Numeric Error Reporting

Table 3-13. Numeric Error Reporting Signals

Signal	I/O	Description
FERR#	O	The **Floating-Point Error** output pin is driven active when a floating-point error occurs. This pin has been included to remain compatible with DOS-oriented systems that use the ERROR output of the Numeric Co-Processor to generate IRQ13 when a Floating-Point error is encountered.
IGNNE#	I	When the **Ignore Numeric Error** input is asserted by external logic, the 80486 microprocessor will ignore a numeric error and continue executing non-control floating-point instructions. When IGNNE# is inactive, the 80486 will freeze on a non-control floating-point instruction if a previous floating-point instruction caused an error. IGNNE# has no effect when the NE (Mask Numeric Error) bit in CR0 is set.

Bus Size Control

Table 3-14. Bus Size Control-Related Signals

Signal	I/O	Description
BS16#	I	When sensed active, the **Bus Size 16** input causes the microprocessor to run multiple bus cycles to complete a transfer from devices that can only provide or accept 16-bits per bus cycle. The state of this pin is sampled at the end of the T1 period to determine the bus size.
BS8#	I	When sensed active, the **Bus Size 8** input causes the microprocessor to run multiple bus cycles to complete a transfer from devices that can only provide or accept 8-bits per bus cycle. The state of this pin is sampled at the end of the T1 period to determine the bus size.

Address Mask

Table 3-15. Address Masking Signal

Signal	I/O	Description
A20M#	I	When the **Address Bit 20 Mask** pin is active, the 80486 microprocessor masks physical address bit 20 (A20) before performing a lookup to the internal cache or driving a memory bus cycle onto the buses. A20M# emulates the address wraparound at the 1MB boundary that occurs on the 8086/8088. This pin should only be asserted by external logic when the microprocessor is in Real Mode.

SL Technology

Table 3-16. Signals Related to SL Technology

Signal	I/O	Description
SMI#	I	The **System Management Interrupt** informs the processor that a system management interrupt service routine, residing in System Management (SM) address space, needs to be performed.
SMIACT#	O	**System management interrupt acknowledge** pin informs external logic that the processor is in system management mode. SMIACT# specifies that the processor is accessing System Management RAM (SMRAM). This pin is used by the system to decode addresses intended for SMRAM.
STPCLK#	I	The **stop clock signal** input indicates that the system wishes to stop the processor's clock input. The processor recognizes on the next instruction boundary. Note that if an interrupt is pending, it will be serviced first before recognizing the STPCLK# signal. Once the processor recognizes STPCLK#, it completes all buffered writes in the write buffers, flushes the instruction pipeline, and generates a stop-grant acknowledge special cycle. The stop-grant acknowledge bus cycle informs external logic that it can stop the processor's clock input.

Boundary Scan Interface

Table 3-17. Boundary Scan Interface Signals

Signal	I/O	Description
TCK	I	**Test Clock**. Used to clock state information and data into and out of the device during boundary scan.
TDI	I	**Test Input**. Used to shift data and instructions into the Test Access Port in a serial bit stream.
TDO	O	**Test Output**. Used to shift data out of the Test Access Port in a serial bit stream.
TMS	I	**Test Mode Select**. Used to control the state of the Test Access Port (TAP) controller.
TRST#	I	Test Reset. Used to force the Test Access Port controller in to an initialized state.

Table 3-18. System Reset Signals

Signal	I/O	Description
RESET	I	The **Reset** input has two important effects on the 80486: 1. Keeps the microprocessor from operating until the power supply voltages have come up and stabilized. 2. Forces known default values into the 80486 registers. This insures that the microprocessor will always begin execution in exactly the same way.
SRESET	I	The **Soft Reset** has the same function as RESET except for the following items: 1. SRESET does not change the system management memory base address (SMBASE). 2. The upgrade processor present (UP#) signal is not sampled on the falling edge of SRESET as is done with RESET. SRESET ensures that the 486DX processor preserves the SMBASE value when executing 80286 compatible code that attempts to change the processor from protected back to real mode (e.g. DOS extenders).

Upgrade Processor Support

Table 3-19. The Upgrade Present Signal

Signal	I/O	Description
UP#	I	**Upgrade Present.** This signal is sampled by a 486 processor to detect if an upgrade processor has been installed. This implementation is used when the system manufacturer provides a separate upgrade socket in which a faster OverDrive processor can be installed. When power is applied to the system, the OverDrive processor asserts its UP# pin to notify the original 486 that it should enter a low power state (upgrade power down mode) and tri-state its outputs.

Chapter 4

The Previous Chapter

The previous chapter defined each of the 486DX processor external pins and described their functions.

This Chapter

This chapter details the operation of the internal data cache including cache-related bus cycles that can be run by the i486DX processor. The interaction between the 486 internal cache and L2 caches are also discussed.

The Next Chapter

The next chapter summarizes and defines the bus transactions that can be run by the 80486 microprocessor, with emphasis on non-cache transactions.

The 486 Caching Solution

The 486 Internal Cache

The internal cache introduced by Intel in the 486 processor provides the additional benefit of limiting the number of memory accesses that the processor must submit to external memory. The 486's internal cache keeps a copy of the most recently used instructions and data (typically referred to as a unified cache). The processor only has to access slow external memory when it experiences an internal cache read miss or a memory write.

The 486 employs a burst transfer mechanism to speed up transfers from external memory. Each internal cache miss forces the processor to access slow external memory. Because the internal cache's line size is 16 bytes, four complete bus cycles would be required to transfer the whole cache line (because the 486 only has a 32-bit data path). The burst transfer capability permits the processor to complete the four transfers faster than it could with zero wait state bus cycles. If the DRAM subsystem utilizes an interleaved memory architecture, the transfers can complete faster than would be possible otherwise.

The Advantage of a Level 2 Cache

Some 486 systems use two levels of cache to improve overall system performance. The internal, or level one (L1), cache provides the processor with the most often used code and data, while the level two (L2) cache provides the processor with code and data that the L1 cache was too small to retain.

Since all information destined for the internal L1 cache must pass through the external L2 cache, the advantage of the L2 cache may not be immediately apparent. If the L2 cache were the same size as the L1 cache (8KB), there would be no advantage. If, however, the L2 cache is substantially larger than the L1 cache, the advantage becomes clear. L2 caches are usually much larger (64KB-512KB) than the 486 L1 cache.

L2 caches improve overall performance because the L1 cache can get information from the L2 cache quickly on most internal read misses. Furthermore, most L2 caches can take full advantage of the 486 burst cycles to accommodate the fastest possible burst transfer.

Consider the case if the L2 cache were sixteen times larger than the internal cache, or 128KB, in size. At a given moment in time, the L2 cache would contain a mirror image of the internal cache's contents and up to fifteen images of the internal cache's previous contents. The net result would be that, as long as the microprocessor is accessing memory locations that are cached in the internal cache, no bus activity to main DRAM need take place. When the microprocessor attempts to access a memory location that isn't cached in the internal cache, an external memory access would be initiated. If the microprocessor had previously accessed the same area of memory, there is a high probability that it will be found in the L2 cache and can be burst back to the microprocessor. Only when a read miss occurs in both the internal and L2 caches would an access to the slow DRAM main memory become necessary.

The 486 with an L2 Look-Through Cache

Figure 4-1 illustrates the relationship of the 80486, the Non-Cacheable Access (NCA) logic, a look-through external (L2) cache, system board memory, and devices that connect to the expansion bus (for example, ISA, MCA or EISA).

Chapter 4: The 486 Cache and Line Fill Operations

When the 80486 must communicate with a device external to itself, it initiates a bus cycle on its local buses. When the L2 cache is implemented as a look-through cache controller, the bus cycle is intercepted by the L2 cache controller.

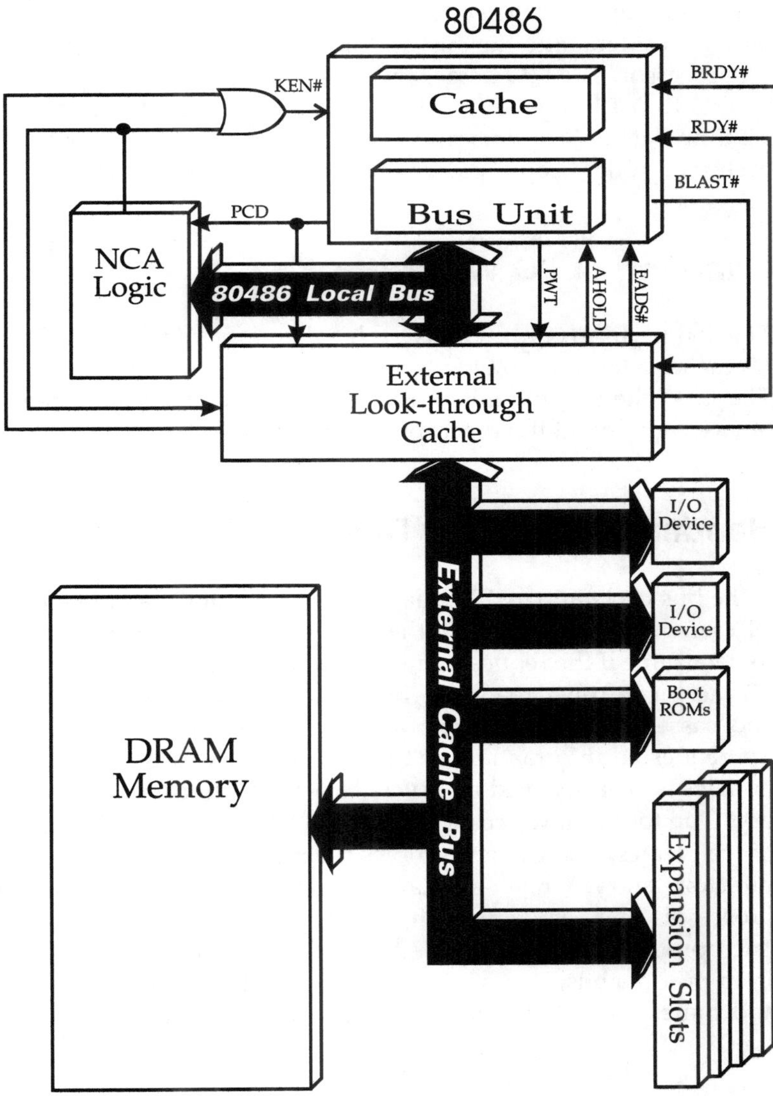

Figure 4-1. The 486 Processor with an L2 Look-Through Cache

Handling of I/O Reads

When the processor executes an IN instruction it performs an I/O read transaction. The L2 look-through cache controller detects the I/O read bus cycle and reinitiates it on the system bus. The target I/O device performs the access and drives data onto the bus, and the L2 cache passes the data back to the microprocessor. The I/O device indicates that valid data is present, the L2 cache asserts RDY# to the 486. The processor samples RDY# at the end of the next T2 time, latches the data and ends the bus cycle. Neither the L2 nor the L1 cache controller keep copies of information read from I/O devices.

Handling of I/O Writes

The 486 performs an I/O bus cycle when executing an OUT instruction. The L2 cache detects the I/O write bus cycle and reinitiates it on the system bus. The L2 cache and the microprocessor end the bus cycle when the target I/O device signals that it has accepted the data.

Handling of Memory Reads

If the bus cycle initiated by the 80486 is a memory read bus cycle (because an L1 cache misshas occurred), the L2 cache controller interrogates its directory to determine if the requested information is present in its cache. If present, the L2 cache controller reads the information from its fast-access cache memory and passes it back to the microprocessor. This is known as an L2 cache hit. If the requested information isn't found in the L2 cache, the L2 cache controller initiates a memory read bus cycle to read the information from DRAM memory. Due to the slow access time of the DRAM, this will involve the insertion of wait states. The L2 cache copies the information into its cache and makes a directory entry, while simultaneously routing the information to the microprocessor and activating the microprocessor's RDY# input. When the microprocessor samples RDY# asserted at the end of T2 time, it reads the data from the data bus, stores it in its internal cache, makes a cache directory entry, and routes the data to the internal unit that originally requested the information.

Handling of Memory Writes

The 486 microprocessor employs a write-through policy. Memory writes are first submitted first to the internal cache which interrogates its directory to determine if a copy of the target memory location's contents is present in its cache. If a copy of the target memory location is not present in the L1 cache, it performs a memory write bus cycle. If present, the new information is first written into the cache to update the entry after which the 486 initiates a memory write bus cycle to also pass the information to external memory. The action taken by the L2 cache controller when it detects the memory write bus cycle is defined by the cache controller type. It may employ either a write-through or a write-back policy:

- A **write-through cache** controller interrogates its directory to determine if it has a copy of the target memory location present in its cache. If present, the cache updates the entry and initiates a memory write bus cycle on the system bus to write the new data to DRAM memory. If the cache doesn't have a copy of the target memory location's contents, it simply initiates a memory write bus cycle on its buses to write the new data through to DRAM memory.
- A **write-back cache** controller interrogates its directory to determine if the information to be updated is present in its cache. If present, the new information is written into the cache to update the entry, but the cache controller does not initiate a memory write bus cycle on its buses to write the new data through to DRAM memory. Instead, the cache's directory entry is updated to indicate that the updated cache line is "dirty" or "modified." This means that the cache now contains the latest information, and that the target memory location in DRAM contains stale data. The cache controller must monitor the system bus to detect memory transfers that access memory locations that contain stale data and take steps to ensure that cache consistency is maintained.

Handling of Memory Reads by Another Bus Master

When another bus master in the system initiates a memory read transaction, the cache subsystem must ensure that cache consistency, or coherency, is maintained. The steps taken by the L2 cache depend on whether the L2 cache employs a write-through or write-back policy.

When a Write-Through Policy is Used

A write-through policy employed by an L2 cache eliminates the cache consistency concerns, since all memory write transactions are passed on through to main DRAM. Furthermore, since the 486 also implements a write-through policy, the L2 cache knows that it always has the latest information. In short, the write-through policy guarantees that a bus master will always obtain valid data when reading from DRAM.

When a Write-Back Policy is Used

A **write-back policy** employed by an L2 cache controller creates the need for the cache controller to monitor memory read transactions to detect when another bus master is reading from a memory location that might contain stale data. If the write-back cache has updated a cache line and set the dirty bit, then the contents of the DRAM memory locations associated with the cache line contain stale data. When another bus master reads from one of these DRAM locations it may read stale data. To prevent this from occurring an L2 write-back cache controller must snoop the system bus to detect memory reads from locations that contain stale data. When this condition is detected the L2 cache must either:

1. Supply the information to the bus master and notify the DRAM controller that it should ignore the access.
2. Back the bus master off (cause the memory read cycle to be suspended) and write the contents of the cache line to memory. When the backoff is removed the bus master can continue the read from memory and be assured of getting valid data.

Handling of Memory Writes by Another Bus Master

When another bus master in the system initiates a memory write transaction, the cache subsystem must ensure that cache consistency is maintained. If a write transaction completes to main DRAM, then any copy of the target location contained in cache will be stale. If the 486 were to perform a read from this location it would receive stale data from cache. The steps taken by the L2 cache controller to prevent this from occurring depends on the write policy that it employs.

When a Write-Through Policy is Used

A write-through policy cache must maintain cache consistency when another bus master writes to main memory. If a bus master performs a write to DRAM and the L2 cache contains a copy of the target memory location, the L2 cache will contain stale data after the write to DRAM completes. In addition, since the L2 cache contains a stale copy of the target memory location, the L1 cache might also have a stale copy. To eliminate the cache consistency problems the L2 cache must snoop the system bus to detect memory writes that access locations that it has a copy of in its cache. The action taken by the L2 write-through cache when detecting a snoop hit during a memory write is either:

1. Invalidate its copy of the target memory locations and pass the snoop address to the 486 so that it can determine if it also has a copy of the target location and, if so, invalidate it.

2. Automatically update its copy of memory location with data written by the bus master (known as snarfing) and pass the snoop address to the 486 so it can invalidate it copy the event of a snoop hit.

When a Write-Back Policy is Used

A write-back policy employed by an L2 cache controller must also monitor memory write transactions to detect when another bus master is writing to a memory location that it has a copy of. The actions taken by a write-back cache depends on the result of the L2 cache snoop as follows:

1. A **snoop hit to a clean line** (one that has not been updated) causes the L2 write-back cache to behave just like the write-through cache. It will either invalidate it copy and send the address to the 486 for snooping, or automatically update its copy of the target location and then send the address to the 486 for snooping.

2. A **snoop hit to a dirty line** (one that has been updated and not written to memory) If the write-back cache has updated a cache line and set the dirty bit, then the contents of the DRAM memory locations associated with the cache line contain stale data.

   Consider what would happen when another bus master writes to a location in memory that the L2 cache has stored in the dirty state. The bus master would update a location in memory that represents some portion of the cache line contained in the L2 cache. Assuming that the cache is not capable of data snarfing (to keep the line updated), it could invalidate the cache line. This, however, would be a mistake. The fact that the line is marked dirty means that some or all of the information in the line is more current than the corresponding locations in memory. The memory write being performed by the current bus master is updating some item in the DRAM memory. Trashing the line from the cache would quite probably trash some data that is more current than that in the memory, leaving stale data in memory. If the cache lets the bus master complete the write and then flushes its line to memory, the data just written by the bus master is over-written by the stale data in the cache line. Either action possibly results in stale data being left in memory. Two possible actions can be taken by the L2 write-back cache to eliminate this potential problem:

- When the L2 cache controller detects the snoop hit to a dirty line it could snarf the data, thereby automatically updating it cache line. The L2 cache would still keep the dirty bit set, since memory might still contain stale data. However, the L2 cache ensures that it has the latest information.

  The L2 cache must also pass the snoop address to the 486 so that it can also perform the snoop. If the 486 experiences a snoop hit it will simply invalidate the cache line.

- The L2 cache could force the bus master off the bus (bus master back off) prior to it completing the write to memory. The cache then seizes the bus and performs a memory write to transfer (write back) the entire cache line to memory. In the cache directory, the cache line is invalidated because the bus master will update the memory cache line immediately after the line is written back, or flushed, to memory. The cache then removes back off, letting the bus master complete the memory write operation. The memory line now contains the most current data.

  The L2 cache must also pass the snoop address to the 486 so that it can also perform the snoop. If the 486 experiences a snoop hit it will simply invalidate the cache line.

The Bus Snooping Process

When a bus master must use the L2 cache's buses to communicate with another device in the system, the L2 cache must release bus ownership. Having surrendered its buses to the new bus master, the L2 cache then snoops the bus. It watches the bus cycles being run by the bus master to see if the bus master is writing new information into a DRAM memory location that the L2 cache has a copy of. If a memory write is detected, the L2 cache controller uses the memory address generated by the bus master to index into its directory. If it determines that the bus master is writing new data into a DRAM memory location that is cached, the cache marks its copy of the information as invalid. In addition, the L2 cache controller will force the 80486 microprocessor to route the memory address generated by the bus master into its internal cache so it can perform the same check and invalidate its cached data if a match is found. The AHOLD (address hold) and EADS# (External Address Strobe) signals are used for this purpose. AHOLD causes the microprocessor to prepare to receive the memory address from the current bus master. EADS# causes the microprocessor to input the memory address and submit it to the L1 cache controller for comparison with its directory.

Summary of the L2 Look-Through Cache Designs

In summary, look-through designs provide performance benefits by:

- reducing system bus utilization since most memory accesses come from cache memory, leaving the system bus free for other bus master's use.
- allowing system concurrency, where both the processor and another bus master can perform bus cycles at the same time, and
- completing write operations in zero wait states using posted writes.

The primary disadvantage of look-through designs is:

- The local CPU's memory requests go first to its cache subsystem to determine if there is a copy of the target location is in its local cache memory. This lookup process delays the request to main memory in the event that the memory request is a cache miss. This delay is commonly referred to as the "lookup penalty)".
- look-through caches are more difficult to design and implement.
- look-through designs are costly.

The 486 with an L2 Look-Aside Cache

Figure 4-2 illustrates a 80486-based system that incorporates a look-aside, rather than a look-through, cache controller. In this configuration, the cache controller sits off to the side and observes each bus cycle initiated by the microprocessor. I/O reads and writes are allowed to proceed without interference. When the microprocessor initiates a memory read or write bus cycle, the L2 cache uses the memory address to index into its directory.

In the case of a memory read, no action is taken by the L2 cache if a read miss occurs. It's up to the memory subsystem to provide a line of information to be stored in both the L1 and L2 caches. When a read hit on the L2 cache occurs, however, the line of information will be burst back to the microprocessor by the L2 cache.

No action is taken by the L2 cache when a write miss occurs. When a write hit occurs, the memory write bus cycle initiated by the microprocessor is allowed to update main memory without interference. While this bus cycle is in progress, the L2 cache uses the data output by the microprocessor to update the cache entry. In other words, the L2 look-aside cache uses a write-through policy when dealing with write hits.

The major advantages of look-aside cache designs are:

- Response time on cache miss cycles. Cache miss cycles complete faster in look-aside caches because the bus cycle is already in progress to main memory and no lookup penalty is incurred.
- Simplicity of design. Look-aside designs need only monitor one address bus, whereas, look-through designs must interface with both the processor bus and system bus.
- Lower cost of implementing due to their simplicity.

The disadvantages of look-aside cache designs are:

- System bus utilization is not reduced. Each access to main memory goes to both the cache subsystem and main memory.
- All memory requests, whether a hit or miss, result in the start of a memory cycle in main memory. This causes a precharge cycle to begin which prevents other devices from accessing main memory until the precharge time has expired.
- Concurrent operations are not possible since all masters reside on the same bus.

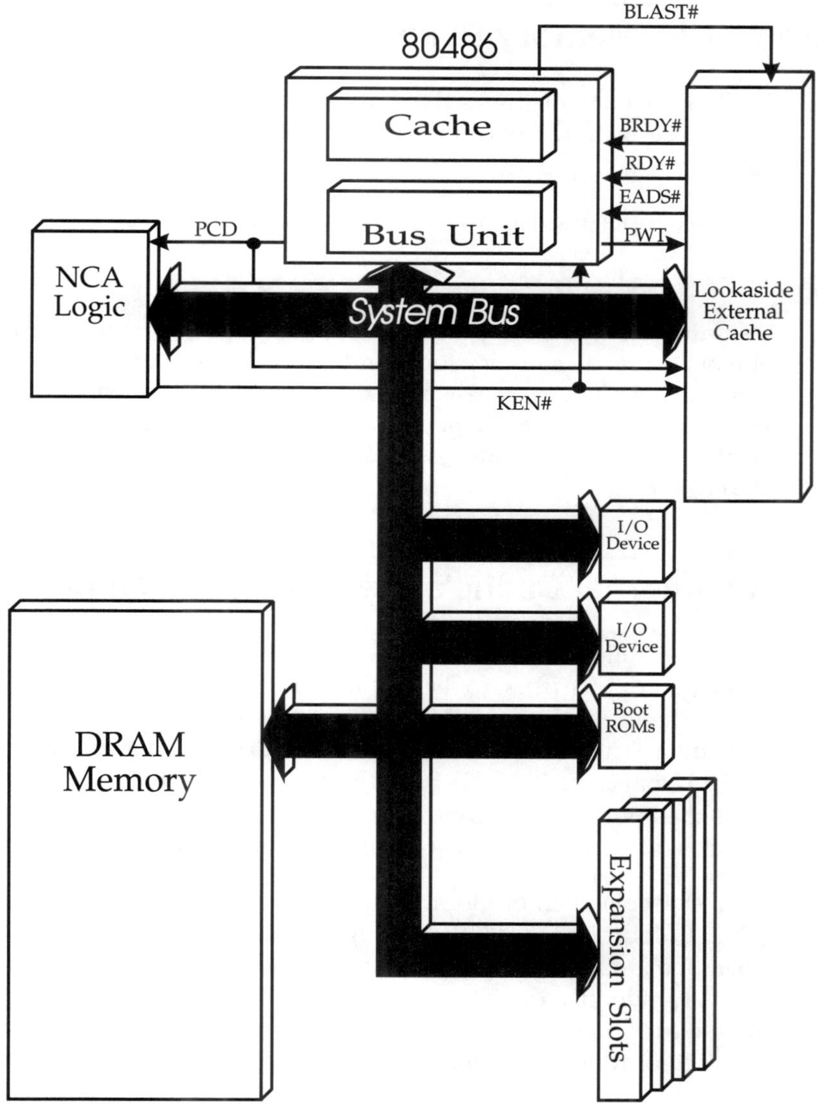

Figure 4-2. The 80486 with a Look-Aside External Cache

Anatomy of a Memory Read

This example demonstrates the sequence of events that occurs when the 80486 microprocessor attempts a memory read operation and the data isn't found in the L1 cache.

In this example, the execution unit is executing the following instruction:

```
MOV  AL,[4025]
```

Assuming that the microprocessor is in either protected or real mode, the data segment starts at memory location 0, and the paging unit is turned off, this would tell the microprocessor to read one byte of information from location 00004025h in the data segment that starts at location 0. In other words, read the byte from memory address 00004025h and place it in the microprocessor's AL register.

The Internal Cache's View of Main Memory

Cache controllers consider the 4GB memory address range of the 80386 and 80486 microprocessors to be divided into areas commonly referred to as pages. The exact size of a page of memory space is cache controller design-dependent. The 80486's internal cache controller divides memory space into 2,097,152 pages of 2048 (2KB) each, numbered 0 through 2,097,151. Furthermore, the internal cache controller considers each 2KB page to be divided into 128 lines (or paragraphs) of 16 bytes each, numbered 0 through 127.

As an example, memory locations 00000000 through 0000000Fh reside in page 0, line 0, locations 00000010 through 0000001F reside in page 0, line 1, etc. When the microprocessor produces a memory address, the upper 21 bits (A31:A11) identify the 2KB page, while the next seven bits (A10:A4) identify the line (or paragraph) within the page. The lower four bits (A3:A0) identify the exact location within the line.

Viewing the example memory address, 00004025h, in this way, the move instruction is attempting to read the contents of the fifth location (A3:A0) in line two (A10:A4) of page eight (A31:A11).

L1 Memory Read Request

The physical memory address, 00004025h, is submitted to the L1 cache controller to see if the requested data item is present in the L1 cache memory. If present, the cache controller immediately fulfills the request from the cache and no bus cycles are necessary on the external buses. If the requested data is not present in the L1 cache, the cache controller submits a memory read bus cycle request to the microprocessor's Bus Unit.

The following paragraphs describe the sequence of events when the requested data isn't present in the cache. This is called a read miss.

The Structure of the L1 Cache Controller

Figure 4-3 illustrates the structure of the L1 cache. There are four banks of cache memory referred to as Way 0 through Way 3. Each of these cache banks consists of 2KB of high-speed static RAM, divided into 128 lines numbered 0 through 127. Each line can hold 16 bytes of information that was retrieved from external memory.

When a line (16 bytes) of information is read from a page of external memory, the cache controller stores the line in one of the four banks of L1 cache memory. Within the selected cache bank, it is stored in the same line number as that which it came from within a page of external memory. The line number also selects the directory entry used to record the new entry. As an example, information from line 12 of any memory page is stored in entry 12 of one of the four cache banks.

Each directory entry has four tag, or page, address fields that are used to record the page number of the memory page that a line of information came from. These Tag fields are numbered from 0 through 3, corresponding to the four cache ways, or banks. When a line of information is read from memory, the cache controller indexes into the directory using the line number. It then examines the current setting of the entry's four Tag Valid bits and compares the portion of the memory address that identifies the page to each of the valid page, or tag, addresses stored in the entry's active Tag fields. If the memory page address compares with any of them, this indicates that the cache has a copy of the addressed line in the same line of the respective cache bank. As an example, if the processor were addressing line 5 in memory page 345, the cache controller would index into entry 5 in the directory and compare the target page number, 345, to each of the valid Tag fields in the entry. If Tag field 2, for instance, contained Tag address 345, the cache controller has a copy of the desired information in line 5 of cache bank 2. The processor can then access the target information.

If the memory page address doesn't compare to any of the Tag fields, this is a cache missand the cache controller issues a memory read request to the Bus Unit to fetch the desired information from external memory. When the requested line of information is fetched from external memory, the cache controller must place a copy of it in the cache and update the affected directory entry to reflect its presence. If all four of the Tag fields are currently in use, the cache controller must determine which of the four lines is the oldest and then overwrite that line with the line of new information. The cache directory entry must then be updated to reflect the presence of the new line of data. Under these circumstances, the current setting of the entry's three LRU bits is used to identify which of the four cache lines is to be used to store the new data from external memory. The line from memory is then stored in the selected cache bank, overwriting the line that was previously stored there. The page number, or tag, of the new memory page is then written into the affected Tag field and the entry's LRU bits are updated to reflect the change. The logic used to update the LRU bits is covered later in this section.

Set the Cache Stage

The purpose of this section is to define the current state of the cache when the example memory read request is submitted to the cache controller. In the example, the target memory address is 0004025h. The cache controller uses the line portion of the address, A10:A4, to index into the directory to entry number two. For the purpose of this discussion, the following conditions are assumed in entry two at this moment in time:

- The LRU bits in entry two are set to 101b.
- All four Valid bits are set to ones. This indicates that the cache currently has copies of line 2 from four separate pages of external memory.
- The Tag 0 field contains the value 200h, indicating that line 2 of Way 0 contains a copy of line 2 from page 200h in external memory.
- The Tag 1 field contains the value A300h, indicating that line 2 of Way 1 contains a copy of line 2 from page A300h in external memory.
- The Tag 2 field contains the value 1000h, indicating that line 2 of Way 2 contains a copy of line 2 from page 1000h in external memory.

- The Tag 3 field contains the value 2314h, indicating that line 2 of Way 2 contains a copy of line 2 from page 2314h in external memory.

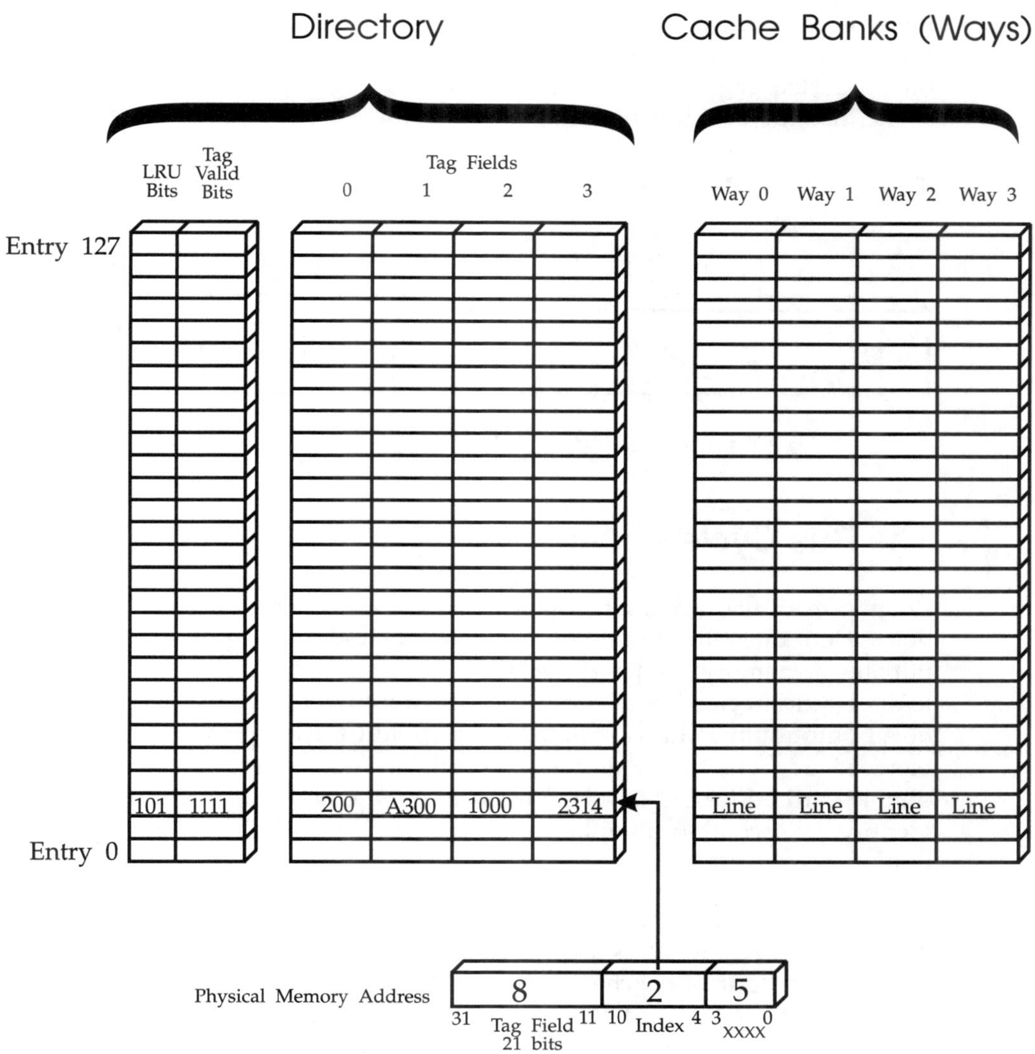

Figure 4-3. The Structure of the L1 Cache

The Cache Look-Up

Figure 4-4 illustrates the internal cache controller's interpretation of the example memory address. A10:A4 contains the value two. This provides the index into the cache directory structure (refer to figure 4-3). Since all four Valid bits in this entry are currently set to ones, the cache controller compares the requested page address, eight, to the four page addresses, or tags, stored in the directory. At this time, none of the stored page addresses matches the requested page address, 8, so a read miss occurs. In other words, the requested data from line two of page eight isn't found in the internal cache.

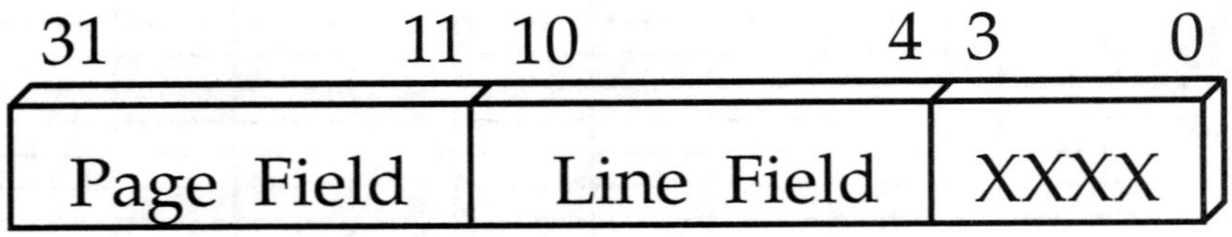

Figure 4-4. Internal Cache Interpretation of the Memory Address

The Bus Cycle Request

When a read miss occurs, the internal cache controller issues a memory read bus cycle request to the microprocessor's bus unit. In response, the bus unit initiates a memory read bus cycle. The 80486 microprocessor strips off the least-significant two bits of the address because the microprocessor has no A0 or A1 output pins. This causes the memory address to be converted to a doubleword address that identifies a block of four locations starting at the doubleword address 00004024h. In addition, the bus unit sets BE1# active to identify the second location in the doubleword, 00004025h, as the target location.

Figure 4-5 illustrates the memory address currently being output by the microprocessor. Figure 4-6 is a timing diagram of the resulting bus cycle. Refer to clock 2 in figure 4-6. When address 00004025h is placed on the address bus, the resultant doubleword address is 00004024h, identifying the block of four memory locations from 00004024 through 0004027h. Since the execution unit has only requested the contents of memory location 0004025h, only the second byte enable line, BE1#, is set active. The following paragraphs provide a detailed description of the entire communications process between the 80486 microprocessor and the memory subsystem.

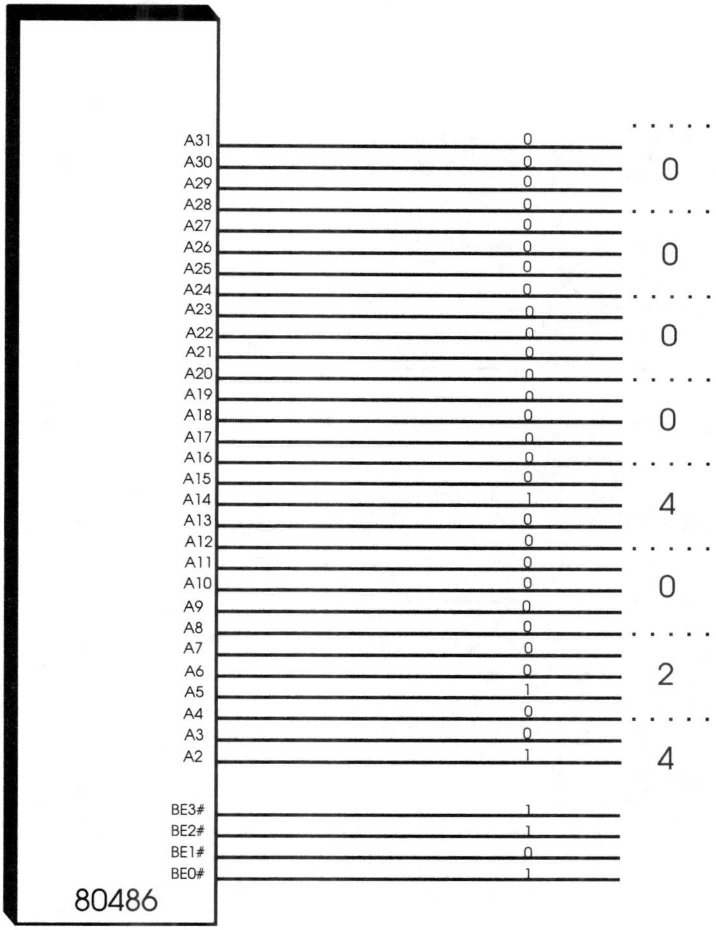

Figure 4-5. Memory Address at the Start of the Bus Cycle

The microprocessor will also set its PCD (Page Cache Disable) output low to indicate to the external memory subsystem that it considers the memory address to be cacheable and would like to receive the entire line containing the requested information. In addition, the microprocessor sets its PWT, Page Write-Through, bit either low or high. PWT is used to instruct a write-back external cache controller in how to handle the memory write. If PWT is low, a write-back controller will update its cache on a write hit, but not main memory. On a write miss, it will write the data to main memory. If PWT is high, a write-back cache controller will update its cache and main memory on a write hit. On a write miss, it will only update main memory.

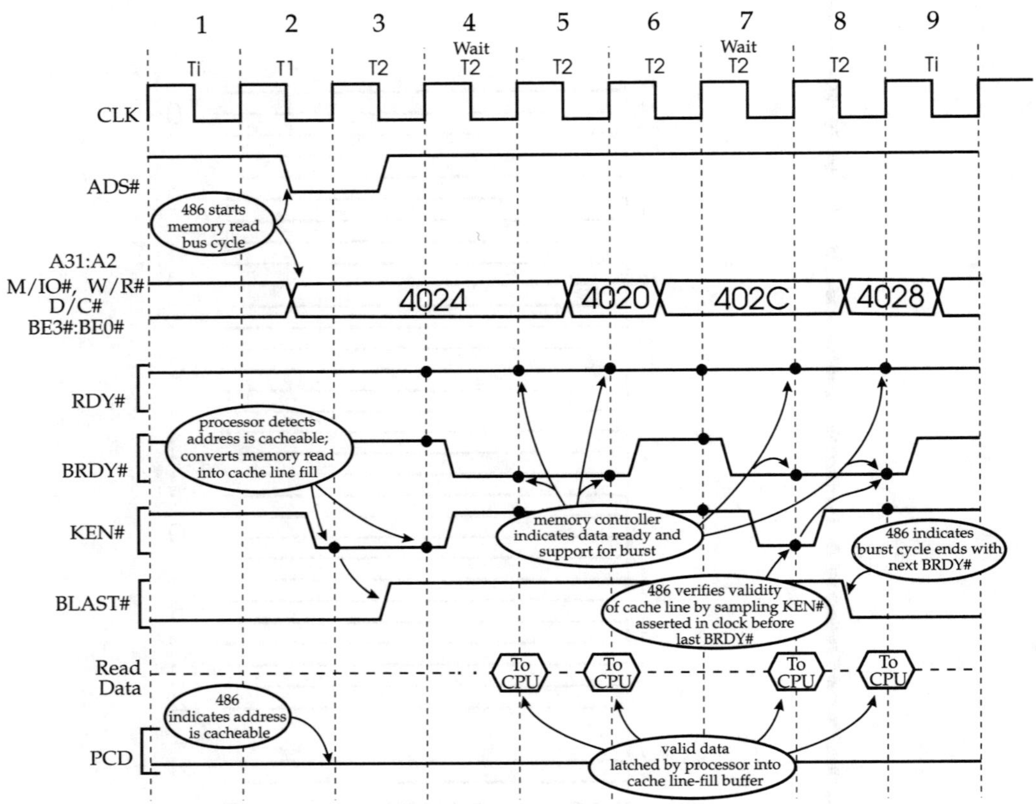

Figure 4-6. Cache Line Fill with Bursting

Memory Subsystem Agrees to Perform a Line Fill

When an internal cache miss has occurred, the microprocessor places the memory address on the address bus and sets PCD low to indicate that it would like to perform a cache line-fill. The NCA logic consists of a programmable memory address decoder on the system board. Each time that the machine is powered up, the NCA logic is automatically programmed to recognize certain configuration-specific memory address ranges as non-cacheable. Information stored in non-volatile memory is used to program the NCA logic.

If the NCA logic considers the memory address on the bus to be cacheable, it should assert the KEN# signal active prior to the end of address time (T1). To determine that memory has agreed to supply a full line of information, the microprocessor must sample KEN# active at the rising-edge of CLK and then sample either RDY# or BRDY# active at the next rising-edge of CLK.

In the example, one wait state is inserted in the first bus cycle while the doubleword starting at memory location 00004024h is read from memory. Assuming that memory address 00004025h is cacheable, the microprocessor samples KEN# active (low) at the end of address time and the again at the end of the first data time (T2). When BRDY# is then sampled active at the next rising-edge of CLK, this indicates to the microprocessor that the addressed memory subsystem has agreed to perform a cache line fill.

Cache Line Fill Defined

Whenever a cache controller incurs a read miss and must therefore "reach" into slower main memory to read the requested data, it attempts to maximize its time on the bus by fetching a larger object than that requested. The larger object is referred to as a line of information. The actual size of a line of information is cache controller design-dependent. The 80486 microprocessor's internal cache controller considers a line to consist of sixteen bytes of information.

Intel refers to a block of sixteen locations as a paragraph of information. A paragraph always starts on address boundaries that are divisible by sixteen (0h, 10h, 20h, etc.). Any memory location resides within a line, or paragraph, of memory space.

In the event of an internal read miss, the microprocessor initiates a memory read bus cycle. At the onset of this bus cycle, the microprocessor is requesting (addressing) only the data item originally requested internally. Once the NCA logic declares the memory address cacheable, however, the microprocessor then expects to receive an entire line consisting of four doublewords of information. The four doublewords are not necessarily sent back to the microprocessor in sequential order starting with the first doubleword in the line, however.

When the microprocessor initiated the bus cycle, it was only requesting somewhere between one and four bytes of information residing within the addressed doubleword. The requested information may be in any of the four doublewords that make up a line of memory space. Upon agreement to perform a cache line fill, the memory subsystem will send back the requested doubleword first, followed by the other three in a pre-determined order. The originally requested doubleword is sent back first so that the execution unit inside the microprocessor may be kept operating at its maximum efficiency. The exact order of transmission of the four doublewords is covered in the section entitled, "The Cache Line Fill Sequence".

Conversion to a Cache Line Fill Operation

In response to the memory subsystem's agreement to perform a cache line fill, (KEN# is sampled active at end of clock 2 in figure 4-6), the 80486 microprocessor turns off its BLAST# (Burst Last) output halfway through the first T2 period. This indicates to the memory subsystem that the microprocessor will perform multiple transfers in order to get the four doublewords from memory. At the end of T2, the microprocessor again samples KEN# active and sets its BLAST# output inactive again. KEN# will not be sampled by the microprocessor again until the start of the last of the four transfers that comprise the cache line fill. The microprocessor's BLAST# output will remain inactive until KEN# is sampled active again at the start of the last transfer. In response to sampling KEN# active again, the microprocessor will turn on its BLAST# output at the midpoint of the last transfer to indicate that the last transfer is in progress.

L2 Cache's Interpretation of the Memory Address

When the microprocessor initially started this bus cycle, it had not yet been converted into a cache line fill operation. In the example, only one of the microprocessor's byte enable outputs, BE1#, is active. When the L2 cache controller and the microprocessor have agreed to perform a cache line fill, however, the cache controller then ignores the actual setting of the microprocessor's byte enable outputs and acts as if all four of them are active. In other words, the entire doubleword will be sent back to the microprocessor. Because the bus cycle has been converted to a cache line fill, the microprocessor will be expecting the entire doubleword despite the actual setting of its byte enable outputs.

The L2 Cache Look-Up

The L2 cache controller uses the memory address to index into its directories and checks for the presence of the requested line of information in its cache memory. In this example, a read miss occurs because the line isn't present in the L2 cache. This means that the L2 cache controller must read the requested line from main memory.

The Affect of the L2 Cache Read Miss on the Microprocessor

Because the first doubleword will not be available for presentation to the microprocessor until it is fetched from the slow DRAM that comprises main memory, one or more wait states are inserted in the bus cycle at this point. When the microprocessor samples RDY# and BRDY# at the end of the first data time (T2), the memory subsystem will not have asserted either of them because it's still reading the first doubleword from DRAM memory. As a result, the microprocessor inserts a wait state (another T2 time slot) in the bus cycle. At the end of this wait state, the microprocessor samples RDY# and BRDY# again to see if the requested doubleword is on the data bus yet.

Organization of the DRAM Main Memory

Refer to figure 4-7. The optimum main memory configuration incorporates three basic elements:

- Interleaved memory architecture. All even-addressed doublewords (A2 = 0) are located in memory bank A, while all odd-addressed doublewords (A2 = 1) are located in memory bank B.
- A 64-bit latch. Incorporating a 64-bit latch as part of the main memory allows it to read two doublewords from memory simultaneously.
- The main memory control logic should be designed to be cache line fill aware. In other words, when informed by the L2 cache controller that a cache line fill is in progress, it will automatically read four doublewords from DRAM and present them to the secondary cache controller in the proper order.

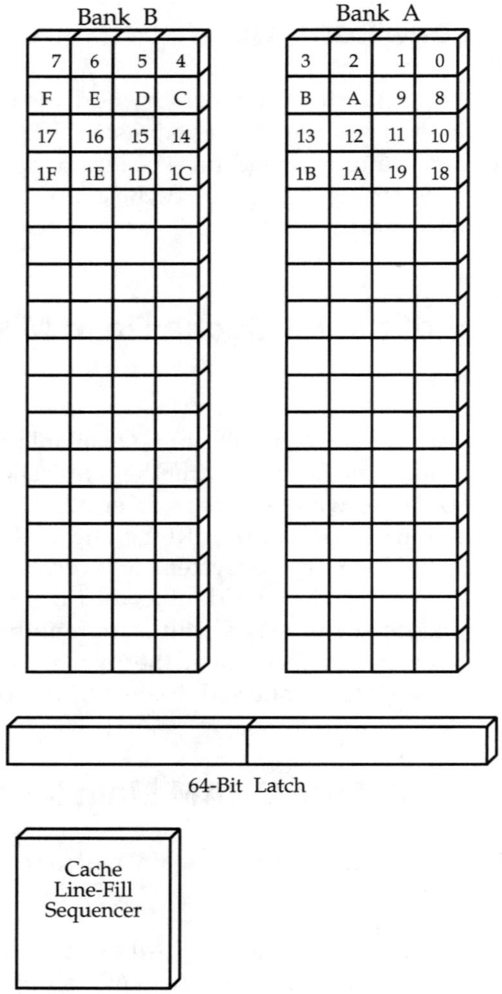

Figure 4-7. 64-Bit Interleaved Memory Architecture

The Cache Line Fill Transfer Sequence

The sequence in which the i486 microprocessor expects to receive the four doublewords that comprise the line is predicated on the 64-bit interleaved memory architecture just described. Table 4-1 defines the sequence of memory addresses output by the microprocessor during a cache line fill operation.

Table 4-1. The Cache Line Fill Transfer Sequence

When Least-Significant Digit of First Address Is	Least-Significant Digit of Second Address Is	Least-Significant Digit of Third Address Is	Least-Significant Digit of Fourth Address Is
0	4	8	C
4	0	C	8
8	C	0	4
C	8	4	0

The First Doubleword Is Read from DRAM Memory

When informed by the L2 cache controller that a cache line fill is in progress, the DRAM main memory subsystem simultaneously reads the first doubleword requested and the adjacent doubleword in the opposite DRAM memory bank. Both doublewords are latched into the 64-bit latch incorporated into the memory subsystem. The memory subsystem then places the requested doubleword on the data bus first.

In the example, the doublewords consisting of 00004024 through 00004027h and 00004020 through 00004023h are simultaneously read and are latched in the memory subsystem's 64-bit latch. The first doubleword, 00004024 through 00004027h, is then placed on the data bus.

First Doubleword Transferred to the L2 Cache and the 80486 Microprocessor

The L2 cache controller latches the first doubleword returning from memory, routes the doubleword to the microprocessor's local data bus and asserts BRDY# (Burst Ready).

At the end of the wait state (the extra T2 at the end of clock 4 in figure 4-6), the microprocessor samples its RDY# and BRDY# inputs to see if the requested data is present on the data bus. When BRDY# is sampled active, it tells the microprocessor two things:

- The first doubleword is present on the data bus.
- The addressed memory supports bursting.

In response, the microprocessor:

- Reads the first doubleword off the data bus and holds it for subsequent storage in the internal cache memory. The information is not stored in the internal cache until the entire line has been retrieved from memory.
- Routes the data originally requested (the contents of memory location 00004025h) to the execution unit. The execution unit then places the byte into the AL register, thus completing the execution of the example MOV instruction.
- Bursts out the second doubleword address, 00004020h, during the next data time and sets all four byte enable outputs active.

Memory Subsystem's Treatment of the Next Three Doubleword Addresses

Since the addressing sequence the microprocessor uses during a cache line fill is predictable based on the initial doubleword address, the L2 cache controller and the memory subsystem may be designed to ignore the subsequent three doubleword addresses output by the microprocessor.

Transfer of the Second Doubleword to the Microprocessor

Upon receipt of the first doubleword, the microprocessor places the second doubleword address on A31:A2 and sets all four Byte Enable lines active (clock 5 in figure 4-6). In the example, the second doubleword address is 00004020h. Since this doubleword has already been read from memory and is present in the 64-bit latch, it is available immediately. The memory subsystem places it on the data bus and it is latched by the L2 cache, placed on the microprocessor's local data bus, and BRDY# is asserted by the L2 cache. At the end of this data time (end of clock 5 in figure 4-6), the microprocessor samples RDY# and BRDY# to see if the second doubleword is present on the data bus. Upon sampling BRDY# active, the doubleword is read from the bus and held for subsequent storage in line 2 of Way 3 in the internal cache. Two of the four doublewords have now been read from memory.

Since BRDY# was active, rather than RDY#, the microprocessor bursts out the third doubleword address during the next data time (clock 6 in figure 4-6).

Memory Subsystem Latching of the Third and Fourth Doublewords

While the 64-bit interleaved memory subsystem was sending the first two doublewords to the L2 cache and the microprocessor, DRAM memory banks A and B were recovering (recharging) from the destructive read process. By the time the second doubleword was sent to the L2 cache and the microprocessor from the 64-bit latch, they are charged up again and ready for another read.

The DRAM memory subsystem reads the next two doublewords from banks A and B simultaneously. In the example, this would be the doubleword comprised of locations 0000402C through 0000402Fh and the doubleword comprised of locations 00004028 through 0000402Bh.

Transfer of the Third Doubleword

The microprocessor outputs the address of the third doubleword with all four Byte Enable outputs active during the next data time (clock 6 in figure 4-6). When the microprocessor samples RDY# and BRDY# (Burst Ready) at the end of the fourth data time (end of clock 6 in Figure 4-6), the memory subsystem will not have asserted either of them because it's still accessing the doubleword from slow DRAM memory. As a result, the microprocessor inserts a wait state (another T2 time slot) in the burst bus cycle. At the end of this wait state, the microprocessor samples RDY# and BRDY# again to see if the requested doubleword is on the data bus yet.

The third doubleword, consisting of locations 0000402C through 0000402Fh, is output onto the data bus from the 64-bit latch. It is stored in the L2 cache, placed on the microprocessor's local data bus and the BRDY# line is asserted by the L2 cache controller. When the microprocessor samples BRDY# active at the end of the current data time (end of clock 7 in figure 4-6), it reads the third doubleword and holds it for subsequent storage in line 2 of Way 3 in the internal cache.

The Beginning of the End

When the third doubleword is placed on the data bus, the Look-through cache controller should assert KEN# (Cache enable). This is necessary to enable the microprocessor's internal cache controller to store the line in its internal cache. The cache controller does not assert KEN# if during the cache line fill it has detected a snoop hit on an address that matches a portion of the line it is currently sending to the 486 internal cache. In other words, another bus master has updated a location in main memory that is contained in the cache line currently being read by the 486. If the 486 is permitted to store the line inside its internal cache it will unknowing have cached stale data.

The microprocessor samples KEN# active at the end of this data time (end of clock 7 in figure 4-6), indicating that the data is valid or fresh.

Transfer of the Fourth and Final Doubleword

The microprocessor places the fourth and final doubleword address on the address bus and activates all four Byte Enable outputs. At the same time, the microprocessor activates its BLAST# (Burst Last) output to indicate that this is the last transfer.

The fourth doubleword, consisting of locations 00004028 through 0000402Bh, is output onto the data bus from the 64-bit latch. It is stored in the L2 cache, placed on the microprocessor's local data bus and the BRDY# line is asserted by the L2 cache controller. The L2 cache stores the entire line and makes a directory entry.

When the microprocessor samples BRDY# active at the end of the current data time, it reads the fourth doubleword and now stores the entire line retrieved from memory page 8, line 2 in line 2 of Way 3 in the internal cache. This completes the cache line fill.

Internal Cache Update

In the example scenario, all four of the Tag fields in entry two are in use (the four Valid bits are active). The cache currently has copies of information from the following areas of main memory:

- Line 2 from page 200h
- Line 2 from page A300h
- Line 2 from page 1000h
- Line 2 from page 2314h

Since all four entries for line two are in use and line two from a new page of memory must be recorded, the cache controller must decide which of the four existent tag fields to overwrite with the new information. Figure 4-8 illustrates the pseudo LRU (Least-Recently Used) algorithm used by the internal cache controller when it must replace a line in the cache.

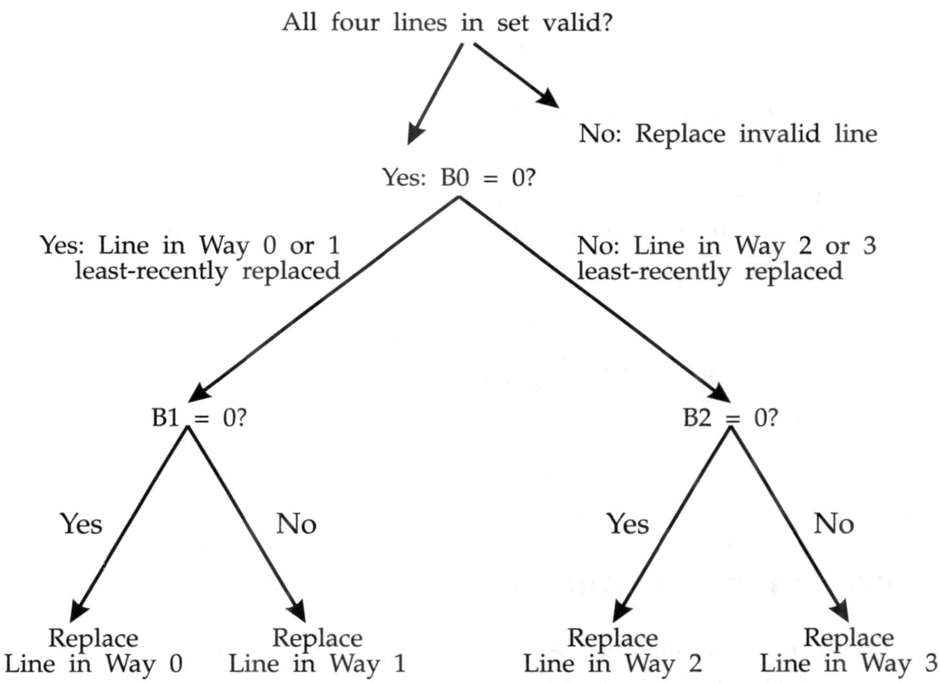

Figure 4-8. The LRU Algorithm

The current setting of the LRU bits is 101b. Since bit 0 and bit 2 are equal to one, the line stored in cache bank (way) three is the entry that will be replaced by the new line. In other words, the line is stored in line two of Way three and Tag three is changed from page 2314h to 8h. The LRU bits are updated to reflect the new ranking of the four entries. If any of the directory entry's four

Valid bits had been 0, the respective Tag field and cache bank would have been used to record this line.

Summary of the Memory Read

If the microprocessor had used regular 80386-style bus cycles to transfer these four doublewords, it would have taken a minimum of twelve PCLK cycles (four 1-wait state bus cycles consisting of three PCLK cycles each). By using the burst-mode transfer, it was accomplished in seven PCLK cycles (3 PCLK cycles for the first transfer, two for the third transfer and one each for the second and fourth). If the requested line of information had been found in the L2 cache, it would only have taken five PCLK ticks because there would not have been a wait state inserted to account for the first slow access to the DRAM that comprises main memory.

The 80486 microprocessor can transfer a doubleword with every cycle of PCLK once it has switched into burst mode. Table 4-2 illustrates the maximum bus transfer rate for the 80486 microprocessor at its presently available clock rates.

Table 4-2. Burst Mode Throughput

80486 PCLK Speed (in MHz)	Burst Mode Throughput
25	100MB/second
33	132MB/second
50	200MB/second

Burst Transfers from Four-Way Interleaved Memory

Memory designs that employ four-way interleaving would result in slightly higher performance if the same cache line fill were performed. Figure 4-9 shows a four-way interleaved memory design that can provide a burst of four consecutive double words, since all four banks are accessed simultaneously. The only performance penalty is the initial access time required of all DRAM banks; therefore, 1 wait-state is inserted a the beginning of the burst transfer.

The example in Figure 4-10 shows a burst transfer as it might look with four-way interleaved memory. Notice that a total of six PCLKs are needed to complete the burst line fill.

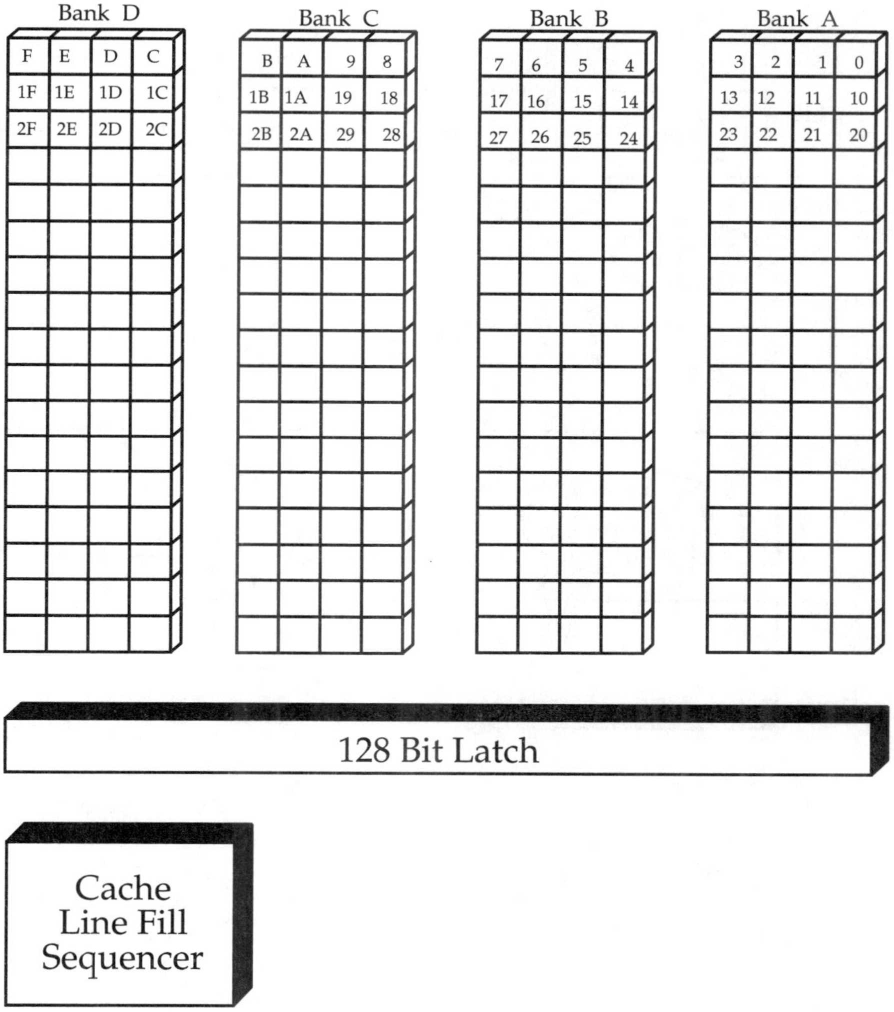

Figure 4-9. 4-way Interleaved Memory Designed to Support Burst Transfers.

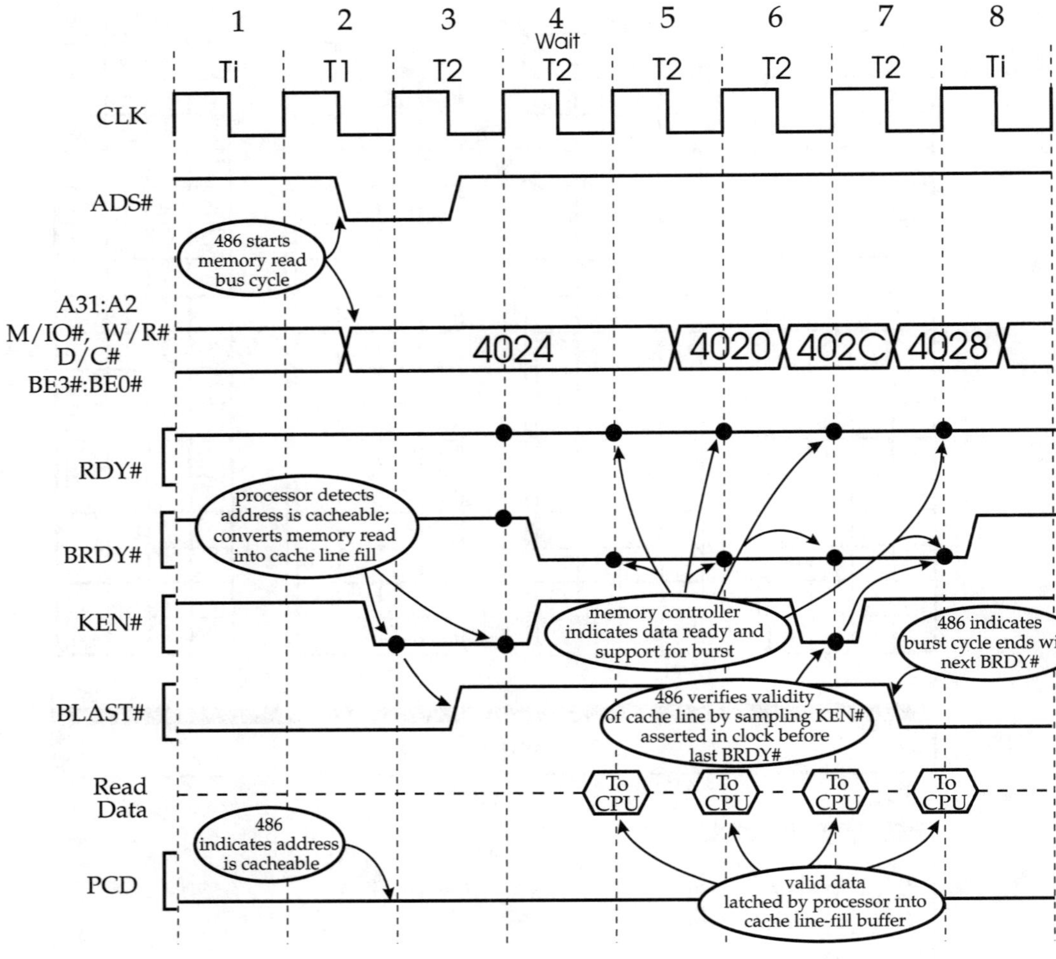

Figure 4-10. Burst Timing from 4-way Interleaved Memory

Burst Transfers from L2 Cache

The highest performance cache line fill occurs when the information requested from memory is found in the L2 cache. Figure 4-11 shows the timing that results when all four doubleword accesses result in cache hits. A total of only five PCLKs are needed to transfer all sixteen bytes.

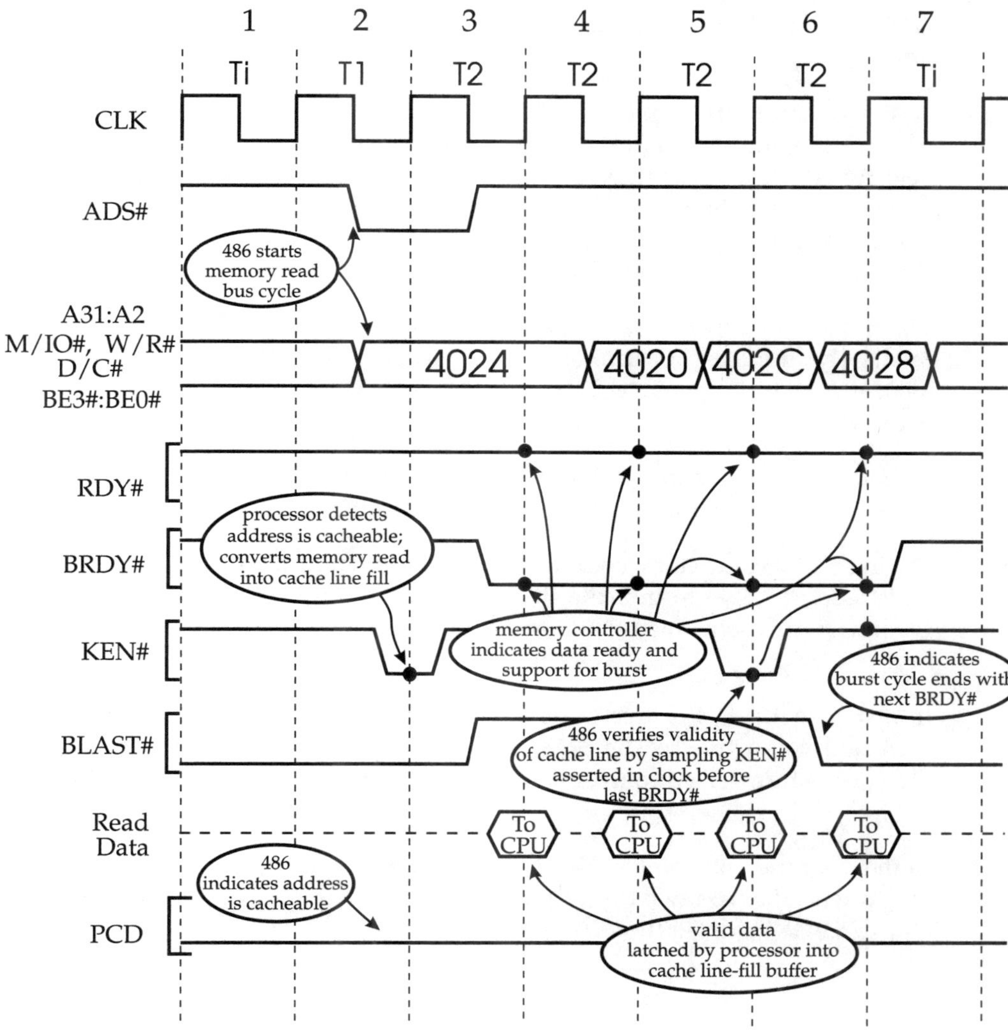

Figure 4-11. Burst Timing from L2 Cache

The Interrupted Burst

In some cases, a memory subsystem may not be able to respond with the four requested doublewords in the order required while performing a burst cache line fill. More time may be required between the reading of some or all of the doublewords. The timing diagram in figure 4-12 illustrates this type of situation.

In this example, the first two doublewords (00004024h and 00004020h) are read from memory in a burst. Since this memory is incapable of supplying the next two doublewords immediately after the first two, the memory logic terminates the first burst by asserting RDY# instead of BRDY# during the third clock of the transfer. This causes the 80486 to "interrupt" the burst, terminating it after the transfer of the doubleword from location 00004020h.

The 80486 still expects the cache line fill to be completed, however, so it immediately initiates a normal bus cycle to fetch the next doubleword (0000402Ch) from memory. This bus cycle is then converted into another burst because:

- the 80486 is keeping BLAST# off to indicate that this isn't the last transfer.
- the memory board returns BRDY# to indicate its ability to burst again.

During the second clock cycle of the newly-initiated burst transfer, the NCA logic asserts KEN# to indicate that the transfer during the next clock will be the last of the cache line fill and the line should then be written to cache memory.

In response, the 80486 asserts BLAST# during the next clock. When BRDY# is then sampled active by the 80486 at the end of the clock cycle, the last doubleword is transferred to the microprocessor and the line is written into cache memory.

In the example, this interruption gives the memory board sufficient time to respond with the next two doublewords needed to complete the cache line fill.

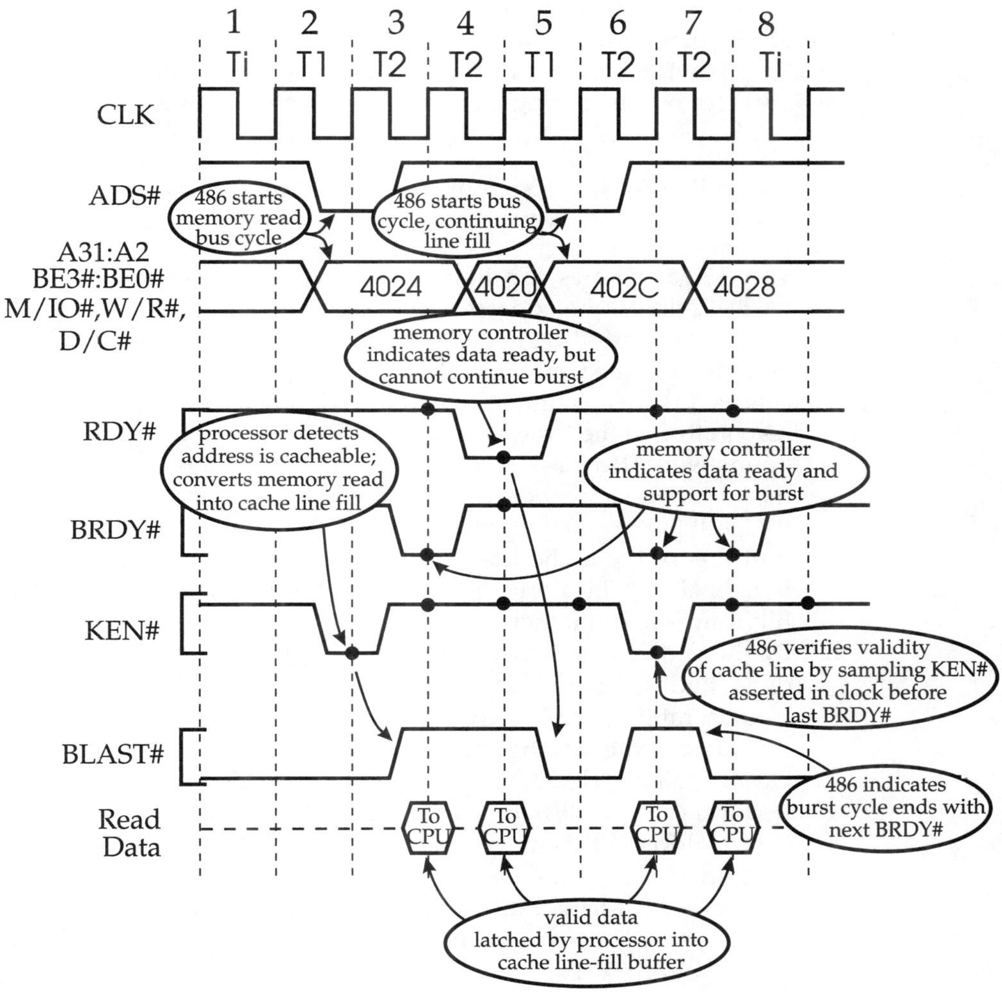

Figure 4-12. The Interrupted Burst

Cache Line Fill Without Bursting

When the 80486 initiates a cache line fill operation, 16 bytes of data must be transferred from the currently addressed memory device into the internal cache. Refer to the timing diagram in figure 4-13 during the following discussion. The numbered steps correspond to the sequence of events illustrated in the timing diagram. This discussion assumes that the addressed memory device is a 32-bit device and the start address is 00004024h. Note that the order of addresses output during a cache line fill isn't what you would expect. This was explained earlier in the section entitled, "The Cache Line Fill Sequence."

The cache line fill involves four separate 32-bit bus cycles and proceeds as follows:

1. The 80486 initiates the first data transfer by placing the first address (00004024h) on the address bus and setting ADS# active in clock cycle 2. Note: when the 80486 initiates the first bus cycle, the bus cycle has not yet been transformed into a cache line fill operation. As a result, the 80486 acts as if this is a regular bus cycle and only asserts the Byte Enables corresponding to the bytes that will be transferred in the currently addressed doubleword. Because of this, during the first transfer of a cache line fill, the addressed device should assume that all four Byte Enables (BE3#:BE0#) are active whether they are or not. During all subsequent transfers of the cache line fill operation, the 80486 will assert the proper Byte Enables. This is only important if the 80486 is performing a cache line fill from 8-or-16-bit memory.
2. By the end of clock cycle 2, the NCA logic should have decoded the address and asserted KEN# (Cache Enable) back to the microprocessor. Upon sampling KEN# active at the end of clock 2, the 80486 will transform the transfer into a cache line fill.
3. During clock cycle 3, the 80486 turns off BLAST# to indicate its ability to perform the overall 16 byte cache line fill transfer as a burst cycle.
4. If the addressed memory doesn't assert BRDY# (because it doesn't support Burst bus cycles) by the end of clock 3, the 80486 doesn't transform the cache line fill operation into a burst cycle. Since the memory addressed in this example doesn't support burst cycles, the memory will assert RDY# instead of BRDY#.
5. When RDY# is sampled active by the microprocessor at the end of clock cycle 3, the 80486 will input the first doubleword transferred from memory locations 00004024-00004027h.
6. Since RDY# was asserted instead of BRDY#, the first bus cycle will terminate and the 80486 will immediately initiate a second bus cycle to transfer the second doubleword from memory.
7. The start address of the second doubleword, 00004020h, is placed on the address bus by the 80486, and ADS# is asserted.
8. KEN# is not sampled by the processor again until the last bus cycle (at the end of clock 8).

9. During clock cycle 5, the 80486 deasserts BLAST# to indicate this isn't the last transfer.
10. Since the memory addressed in this example doesn't support burst cycles, the memory will assert RDY# instead of BRDY# to indicate the availability of the addressed data.
11. When RDY# is sampled active by the microprocessor at the end of clock cycle 5, the 80486 will input the second doubleword transferred from memory locations 00004020-00004023h.
12. Since RDY# was asserted instead of BRDY#, the second bus cycle will terminate and the 80486 will immediately initiate a third bus cycle to transfer the third doubleword from memory.
13. The start address of the third doubleword, 0000402Ch, is placed on the address bus by the 80486, and ADS# is asserted.
14. KEN# is not asserted by the addressed memory again until the last bus cycle.
15. During clock cycle 7, the 80486 again deasserts BLAST# to indicate this isn't the last transfer.
16. Since the memory addressed in this example doesn't support burst cycles, the memory will assert RDY# instead of BRDY# to indicate the availability of the addressed data.
17. When RDY# is sampled active by the microprocessor at the end of clock cycle 7, the 80486 will input the third doubleword transferred from memory locations 0000402C-0000402Fh.
18. Since RDY# was asserted instead of BRDY#, the third bus cycle will terminate and the 80486 will immediately initiate the fourth and final bus cycle to transfer the fourth doubleword from memory.
19. The start address of the fourth doubleword, 00004028h, is placed on the address bus by the 80486, and ADS# is asserted.
20. KEN# is asserted by the NCA logic during T1 of the last bus cycle. KEN# must be sampled active at the end of the clock cycle prior to RDY# of the last bus cycle in order for the line to be written into internal cache memory.
21. During clock cycle 8, the 80486 keeps BLAST# asserted to indicate this is the last transfer.
22. Since the memory addressed in this example doesn't support burst cycles, the memory will assert RDY# instead of BRDY# to indicate the availability of the addressed data.
23. When RDY# is sampled active by the microprocessor at the end of clock cycle 9, the 80486 will input the fourth doubleword transferred from memory locations 00004028-0000402Bh, and all four doublewords (16 bytes) are copied into the target line in cache memory.

24. Since RDY# was asserted instead of BRDY#, the fourth bus cycle will terminate, thus completing the non-burst cache line fill operation.

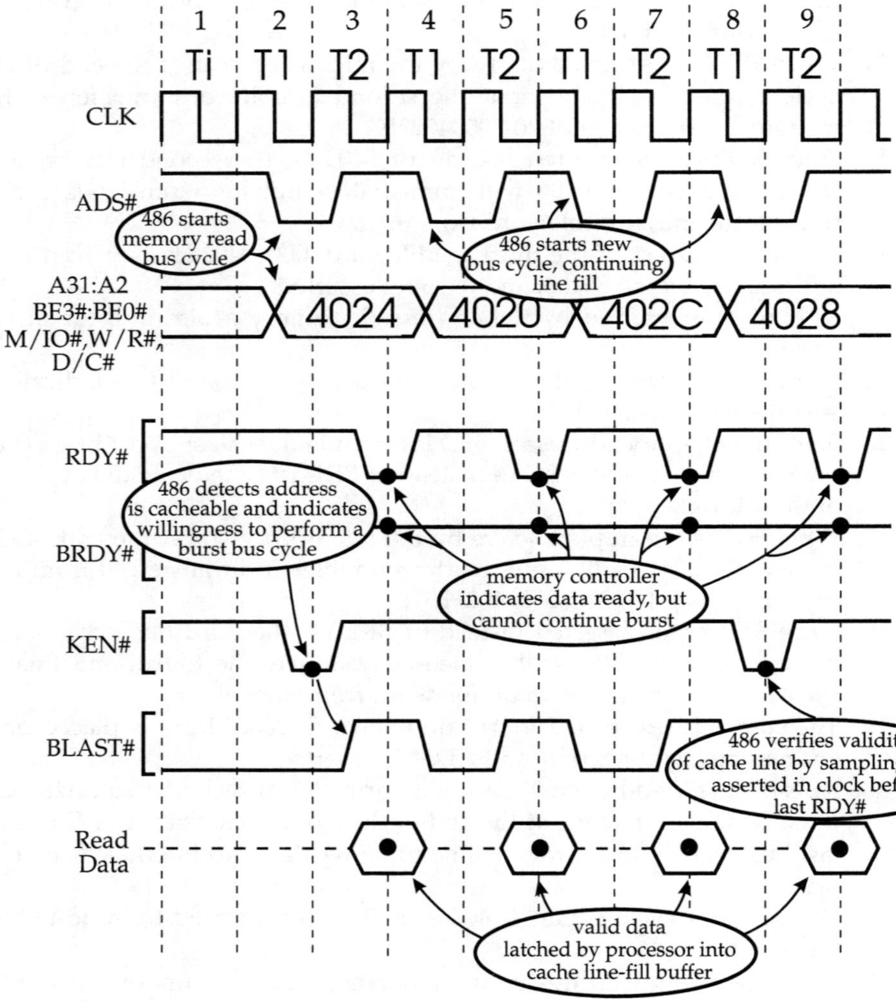

Figure 4-13. Non-Burst Cache Line Fill

Internal Cache Handling of Memory Writes

The internal cache controlleruses a write-through policy to handle write hits. When the microprocessor initiates a memory write operation, the cache controller uses the index, or line, portion of the physical main memory address to identify the proper directory entry. If any of the four Tag Valid bits are set, it then compares the tag, or page, portion of the memory address to the respective tag fields in the directory entry. If one of them matches, it is called a write hit. The cache controller will perform a write-through.

This means that the cache controller updates the data stored in the cache memory location and immediately commands the Bus Unit to perform a memory write bus cycle on the external buses. This will update the external memory location as well as the cache memory location. In this way, the data in the internal cache always mirrors that in external memory.

Invalidation Cycles (486 Cache Snooping)

When a bus master other than the 80486 performs a write to main memory, the 80486's internal cache must be made aware of the change. The internal cache may have a copy of this location's data. If an external bus master then alters this main memory location's contents, this means that the respective line in the internal cache no longer accurately reflects the true contents of the memory location.

In order to maintain cache coherency, the 80486 incorporates a bus "snooping" mechanism that can watch the address bus when an external bus master is writing to main memory. This is implemented with two 80486 pins:

- AHOLD (Address Hold). External logic will set AHOLD active in response to a main memory write in progress by another bus master. In response to AHOLD, the 80486 will immediately relinquish control of its address bus.
- EADS# (External Address Status). The external logic then asserts EADS# to indicate that the external bus master has placed a valid memory address on the address bus. A31:A4 are now used as inputs to the 80486 so the internal cache controller can observe the main memory address being written to. This address is used to perform a lookup in the cache controller directory. If the cache controller senses that the contents of the main

memory location being written to is also contained in a line in the internal cache, the respective line in the internal cache will be marked invalid because its contents no longer accurately reflect the contents of main memory.

This internal snoop is called a cache invalidation cycle since the only purpose of performing a snoop is to direct the processor to invalidate its copy of the cache line if a snoop hit occurs. Figure 4-14 illustrates the cache invalidation cycle.

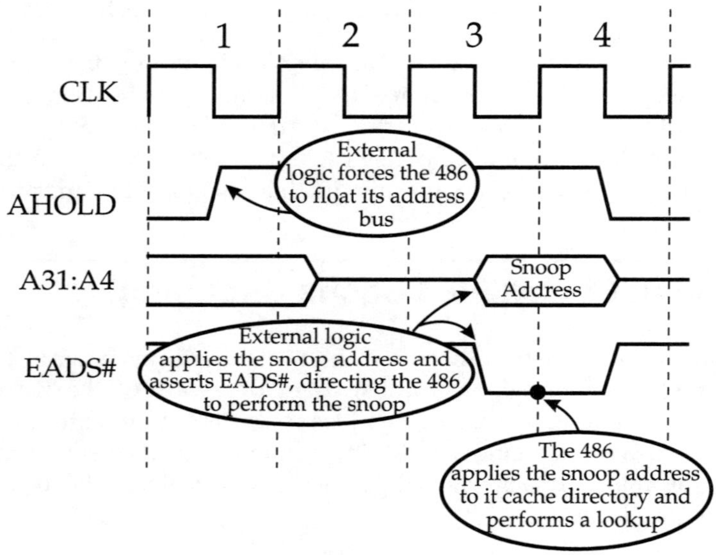

Figure 4-14. Cache Invalidation Cycle

L1 and L2 Cache Control

The internal cache is controlled by a number of factors listed below. Note that the following section references are in the chapter entitled "Summary of Software Changes."

- The CD and NW bits in CR0. These two bits are discussed in the section entitled, "Control Register 0 (CR0)."
- The PCD bit in CR3. If paging is not enabled, the PCD bit from CR3 supplies the microprocessor's PCD output during a memory read bus cycle.

PCD is almost always set to zero by a non-paging operating system, forcing the 80486 to consider all of memory address space to be cacheable. When paging is enabled, PCD is supplied from the addressed Page Table entry. See the section entitled, "Virtual Paging."

- The FLUSH# input to the microprocessor. When active, FLUSH# causes all of the internal cache controller's Tag Valid bits to be cleared. The method used to enable or disable the FLUSH# line is system-dependent.
- Execution of the INVD instruction. See the section entitled, "Instruction Set Enhancements."
- Execution of the WBINVD instruction. See the section entitled, "Instruction Set Enhancements."

The L2 cache can be controlled via the 486 in the following ways:

- The FLUSH# control line. When active, FLUSH# causes all of the L2 cache controller's Tag Valid bits to be cleared.
- Execution of the INVD instruction. See the section entitled, "Instruction Set Enhancements."
- Execution of the WBINVD instruction. See the section entitled, "Instruction Set Enhancements."
- The state of the microprocessor's PWT output. If paging is not enabled, the PWT bit from CR3 supplies the microprocessor's PWT output during a memory write bus cycle. When paging is enabled, PWT is supplied from the addressed Page Table entry. The state of the PWT signal line instructs a write-back L2 cache on how to handle memory writes (using either a write-back or write-through policy). See the section entitled, "Virtual Paging."

Chapter 5

The Previous Chapter

The last chapter detailed the operation of the internal data cache, including cache-related bus cycles that can be run by the i486DX processor. The interaction between the 486 internal cache and L2 caches were also discussed.

This Chapter

This chapter summarizes and defines the bus transactions that can be run by the 80486 microprocessor, with emphasis on non-cache transactions.

The Next Chapter

The next chapter discusses the SL Technology features implemented in the 486DX family of processors.

Overview of 486 Bus Cycles

The 486DX processor is capable of performing a variety of bus cycle types that are defined by the processor when it outputs the bus cycle definition pins at the beginning of the bus cycle (see next section). In addition, the bus cycle type may be further defined by software or the assertion of signals. For example, as described in the previous chapter, a memory read transfer can be converted into a burst cache line fill transfer by the assertion of KEN# and BRDY# and deassertion of RDY#. The following list defines the bus cycle transactions that the 486 can perform:

- Interrupt Acknowledge cycles
- Special cycles
- Single I/O and Memory bus cycle transfers (single item transferred)
- Cacheable burst bus cycle transfers from 32-bit memory
- Invalidation Cycles (cache snoops)

- Non-cacheable burst bus cycle transfers
- Locked transfers
- Pseudo-locked transfers
- Transfers with BOFF# asserted

The following sections detail each of these transaction types, except cacheable burst read transfers from 32-bit memory and invalidation cycles (refer to the chapter entitled, "The 486 Cache and Line Fill Operations").

Bus Cycle Definition

The processor outputs its bus cycle definition lines at the beginning of the bus cycle. These lines notify external logic of the type of transaction that the processor wishes to perform. Table 5-1 illustrates the seven transactions types that the 486 can perform. External logic decodes these lines and generates the appropriate commands that are native to a given expansion bus.

Table 5-1. The 486 Bus Cycle Definition Lines Transaction Types

M/IO#	D/C#	W/R#	Bus Cycle Type
0	0	0	Interrupt Acknowledge
0	0	1	Special Cycle
0	1	0	I/O Read
0	1	1	I/O Write
1	0	0	Code Read
1	0	1	Reserved
1	1	0	Memory Data Read
1	1	1	Memory Data Write

Interrupt Acknowledge Bus Cycle

Like previous x86 processors, the 486 performs two back-to-back interrupt acknowledge bus cycles in response to its maskable interrupt request pin (INTR) being asserted. These back-to-back cycles are performed as a locked pair, during which the processor ignores its hold request (HOLD) input.

The interrupt vector is returned during the second cycle over D7:D0, while data returned by the system during the first cycle is ignored. The state of A2 permits external logic to differentiate between the first (A2=1) and second (A2=0) interrupt acknowledge cycles. The 486 processor also inserts four idle states between the first and second cycle, to allow I/O recovery time for the 8259 interrupt controller.

Special Cycles

The 486 processor supports five types of special cycles. Table 5-1 shows the state of the bus cycle definition lines during a special cycle, while table 5-2 lists the types of special cycle supported. To determine the type of special cycle being run, the system must decode byte enable lines BE3#:BE0# and A2 as shown in table 5-2.

Table 5-2. Special Cycle Decoding

Special Cycle Type	BE3#	BE2#	BE1#	BE0#	A2
Shutdown	1	1	1	0	0
Flush	1	1	0	1	0
Halt	1	0	1	1	0
Stop Grant Acknowledge*	1	0	1	1	1
Write-back	0	1	1	1	0

* Not performed by the original i486DX and i486SX processors.

Shutdown Special Cycle

The 486 processor performs a shutdown special cycle when a triple fault condition occurs. The 486 processor detects a triple fault and goes into a shutdown cycle if while handling a double fault exception and another fault is detected. The processor stops all execution after the shutdown special cycle is performed. Note that the NMI signal can cause the 486 processor to recover from a shutdown condition, without resetting the processor.

Flush Special Cycle

The flush special cycle is generated in conjunction with two instructions:

- **INVD** (invalidate instruction) — When the INVD instruction executes, the processor sets all cache entries to the invalid state and runs the flush special cycle. A flush special cycle notifies external logic that all internal cache lines have been invalidated, and tells the L2 cache (if present) that it should also invalidate its cache entries.
- **WBINVD** (write-back and invalidate) — When the WBINVD instruction executes, the 486 processor sets all cache entries to the invalid state and performs two special cycles: the write-back special cycle followed by the flush special cycle. The intent of the WBINVD instruction is to notify an L2 cache that employs a write-back policy to flush, or write-back, all modified data to memory prior to invalidating its cache entries. Once all lines are written back the processor runs a write back special cycle followed by a flush special cycle. (See also "Write-back Special Cycle.")

Halt Special Cycle

As with earlier Intel X86 processors, the halt special cycle is driven when a HLT instruction is executed. The system must return RDY# to the processor in recognition of a halt special cycle. The 486 processor leaves the halt state when any of the following signals are asserted:

- INTR (when maskable interrupts are enabled)
- NMI

- RESET

Stop Grant Acknowledge

The stop grant special cycle is performed when the processor recognizes the STPCLK# (stop clock) interrupt. As shown in table 5-2, BE3#:BE0# are the same for the stop grant acknowledge and halt special cycles, while the state of address line two (A2) distinguishes between these two types of special cycle. Note that the system must return either RDY# of BRDY# before the processor will enter the stop grant state. (See the chapter entitled "SL Technology" for additional information.)

Write-Back Special Cycle

The write-back special cycle is run when the WBINVD instruction executes to notify external logic that the level two (L2) cache should write-back all modified (dirty) lines to external memory. The processor invalidates its internal cache entries and performs the write-back special cycle followed by the flush special cycle. This forces the L2 cache to, first, write-back its modified data and, second, invalidate all of its cache line entries.

Non-Burst Bus Cycles

The 486 microprocessor performs non-burst bus cycles when a single item of information is to be transferred to or from the target device. The data item transferred may be one, two, three, or four bytes in size, depending on the instruction being executed and the size of the target device.

As with the 80386, the fastest non-burst transfer requires two processor clock cycles. Figure 5-1 illustrates three back-to-back non-burst non-cacheable transfers. Note that the processor will always perform a single cycle transfer when RDY# is returned asserted for the first data item.

Figure 5-1 illustrates the processor performing three bus cycles each of which transfer a single byte of data. Since the processor knows that a single byte is to be transferred, it keeps BLAST# asserted (because these bus cycles are not candidates for bursting).

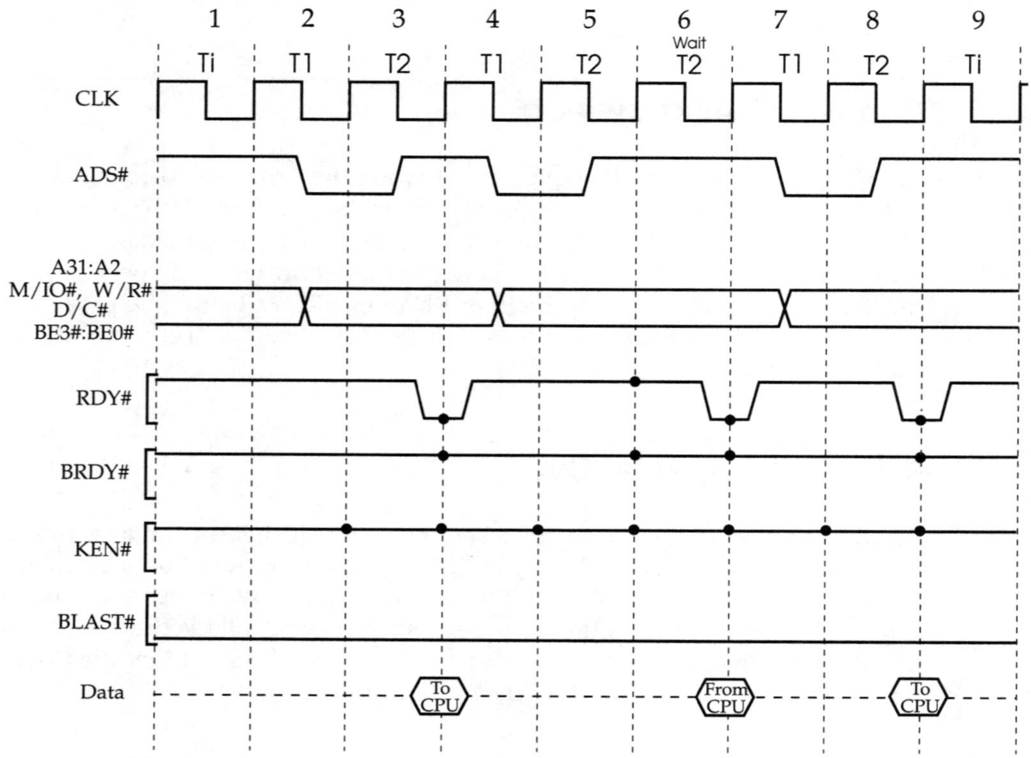

Figure 5-1. Example of Non-Burst Cycle Timing

Transfers with 8-,16-, and 32-bit Devices

Address Translation

The 486 processor's address bus consisting of A31:A2 and BE3#:BE0# are designed to address 32-bit devices. The typical address required by other devices in the PC environment depends on their size as follows:

16-bit devices — A23:A1 and BHE#, BLE# (Bus High, Low Enable)
8-bit devices — A19:A0

Logic external to the processor must translate the address to the form expected by these different size devices as shown in figure 5-2. Notice that 32-bit devices require no translation of the address output by the 486 processor. This means that no translation is needed for the external cache and main memory subsystem since they are 32-bit devices. The address translation is typically done in the expansion bus control logic for smaller devices that are integrated onto the system board or residing in expansion slots.

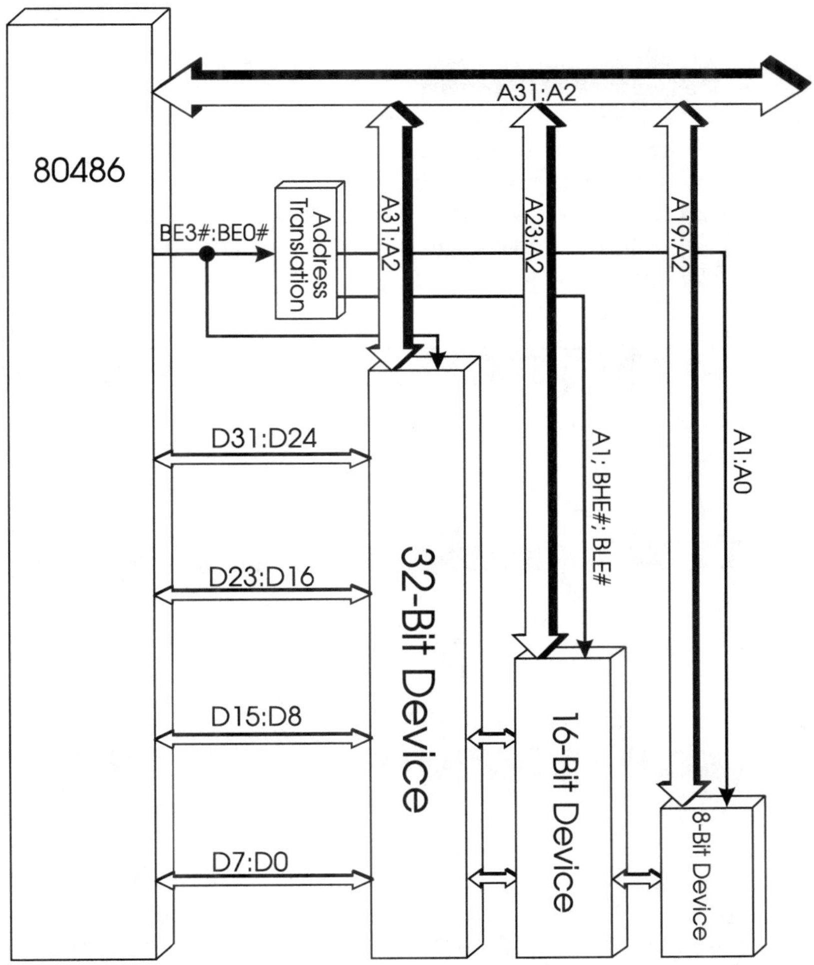

Figure 5-2. Address Translation for 8, 16, and 32-bit Devices

Data Bus Steering

External logic must also ensure that information read from and written to 8- or 16-, devices be transferred over the correct data path(s). Since smaller devices such as 8-bit devices connect to the lower data paths only and since the 486 processor when reading from a device expects data from given locations to be transferred over their respective data paths, data from a specified address location must be directed or steered to the path over which the 486 processor expects it. Conversely, when the 486 processor writes data to a device, it assumes that the device is connected to all 4 data paths (that is, a 32-bit device). However, if the device is smaller that 32-bits the data paths used by the 486 processor may not connect to the smaller devices, and again the data must be steered to the correct path. This is accomplished with a series of transceivers that can pass data from one path to another. Figure 5-3 illustrates the data path transceivers and latches typically implemented in 486 expansion bus chip sets.

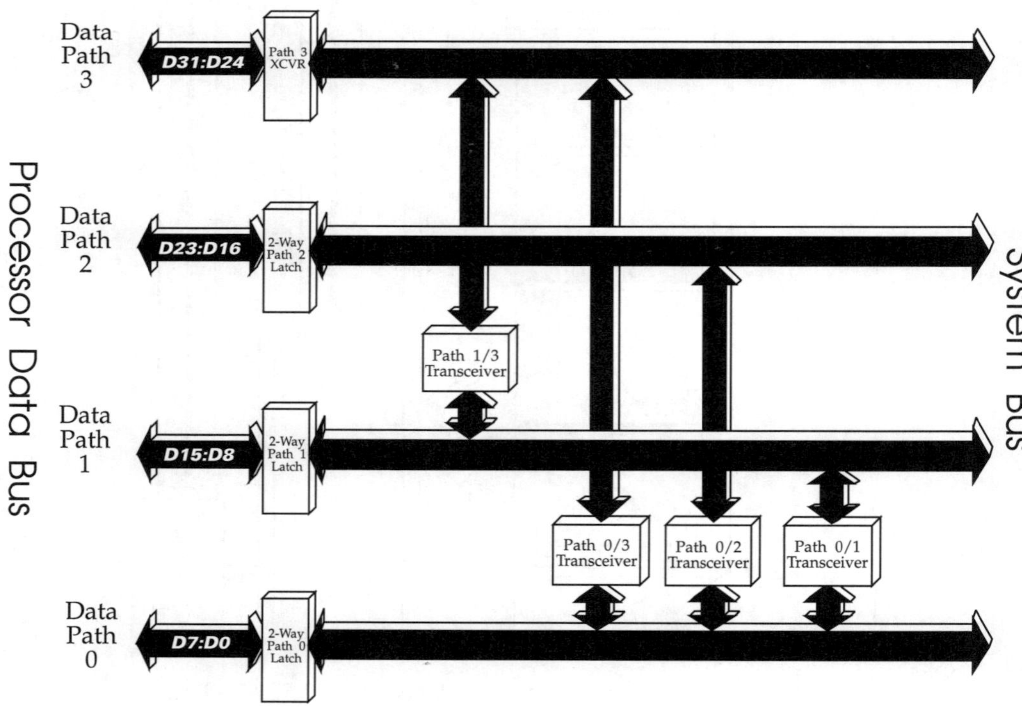

Figure 5-3. System Logic Used to Perform Data Bus Steering

Non-Cacheable Burst Reads

When the 486 microprocessor attempts to perform non-cacheable bus transactions that will require multiple bus cycles to complete, it may be able to perform that transaction using the burst mechanism. Any CPU read transaction that requires multiple bus cycles to complete is a candidate for a burst bus cycle. Examples include:

- misaligned transfers
- instruction prefetches
- 64-bit floating-point reads
- reads from 8- or 16-bit devices

When the 486 starts a bus transaction that may take more that one bus cycle to complete, it deasserts the burst last (BLAST#) signal to notify external logic that it is willing to perform a burst transaction. The target device responds by returning BRDY# if it supports burst transfers. A target device that does not support burst transfers will return RDY# to the processor (rather than BRDY#), causing the bus cycle to terminate with a single transfer. The processor then must perform additional bus cycles until the entire transaction is completed.

Figure 5-4 illustrates the processor performing a burst transfer as a result of a 64-bit floating-point read from 32-bit memory. The processor recognizes that more than one bus cycle will be required to complete the transaction, and therefore, it deasserts BLAST# during the first data phase (T2), mid way through clock 3. Since the processor samples both RDY# and BRDY# deasserted at the end of clock 3, the 486 keeps BLAST# deasserted (because it has not yet determined whether the target device supports burst). At the end of the next data phase (clock 4), the processor sample RDY# deasserted and BRDY# asserted. The processor now knows that target memory supports burst. In response, the processor continues the bus cycle, and asserts BLAST# since there is only one more 32-bit transfer required to complete the 64-bit floating-point read. When BRDY# is asserted again (end of clock 5) the processor ends the bus cycle.

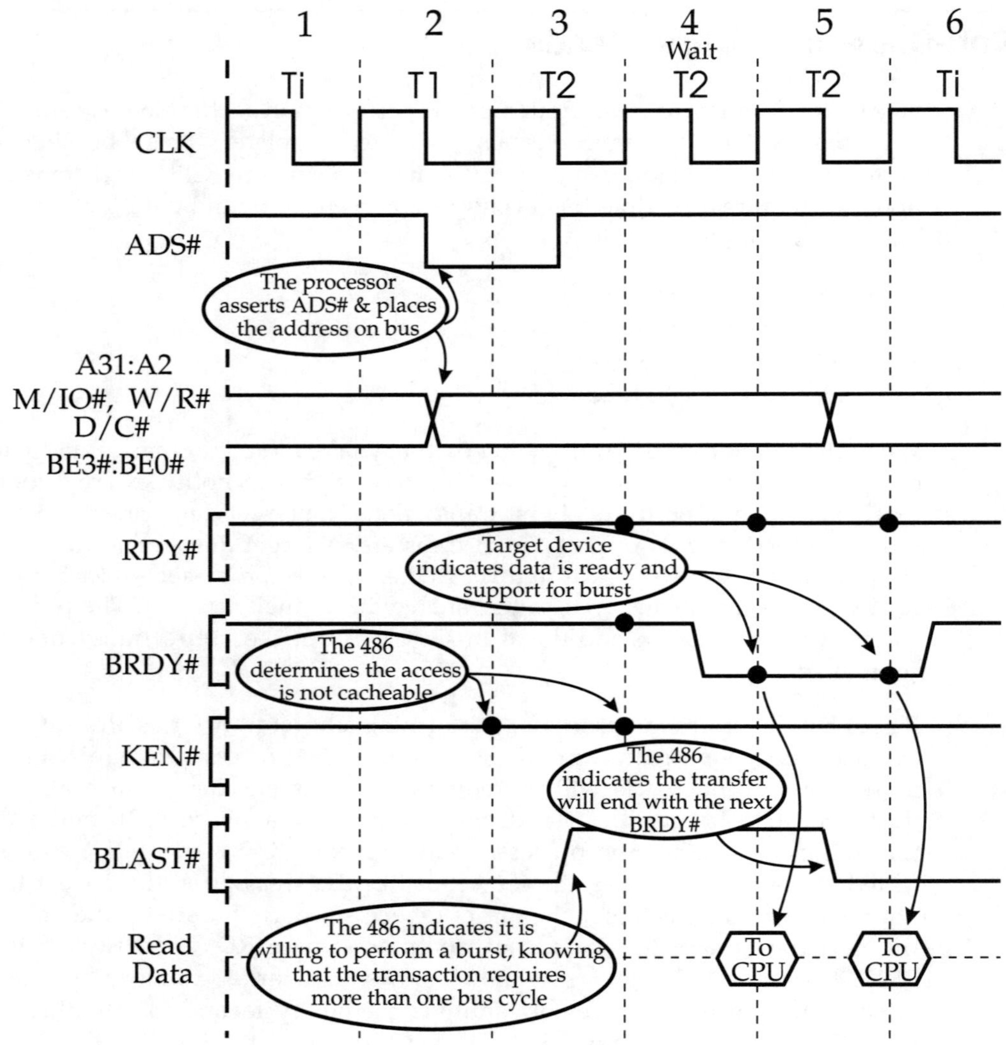

Figure 5-4. Non-Cacheable Burst Read Bus Cycle

Non-Cacheable Burst Writes

The 486 processor can perform burst write bus cycles with a maximum burst size of 4 bytes and can only be performed when either BS16# or BS8# are asserted. Write transactions that the 486 may be able to perform burst transactions on include:

- 32-bit write to a 16-bit device
- 32-bit write to an 8-bit device
- 16-bit write to an 8-bit device

Figure 5-5 illustrates a burst write bus cycle that results from a 32-bit write transaction to an 8-bit device. The processor samples BS8# asserted at the end of the address phase (clock 2). This informs the processor that the 32-bit write transaction will require four transfers and that a burst bus cycle is possible. Midway through the first data phase (clock 3) the 486 deasserts BLAST# to indicate its willingness to perform a burst bus cycle. Since the target memory device supports burst, it asserts BRDY# informing the processor to continue the bus cycle. In response, the 486 processor keeps BLAST# deasserted and continues to sample RDY# and BRDY# at the end of each data phase. When BRDY# is sampled asserted again at the end of clock 5, the processor recognizes that only one byte remains to be written to the 8-bit device. Therefore, midway through clock 6 the 486 asserts BLAST# indicating that only one transfer remains. When BRDY# is sampled asserted again at the end of clock 6, the burst bus cycle is terminated.

The address output by the processor identifies a 4-byte block of locations to which the processor is writing data. When the processor recognizes that an 8-bit device resides within the target locations, it must increment the address using BE3:BE0#. Initially, the bytes enables are all asserted, however when the 8-bit device asserts BRDY# the processor knows that the low byte of the doubleword has been accepted by the device and that three bytes remain to be transferred. For the next transfer, the processor asserts BE3#:BE1# (midway through clock 4), thereby addressing the next three bytes. Once again the target device accepts the low byte and asserts BRDY#. The processor then addresses the remaining two bytes by asserting BE3#:BE2. After the third BRDY# is sampled asserted by the 486, is address the final byte by asserting only BE3#.

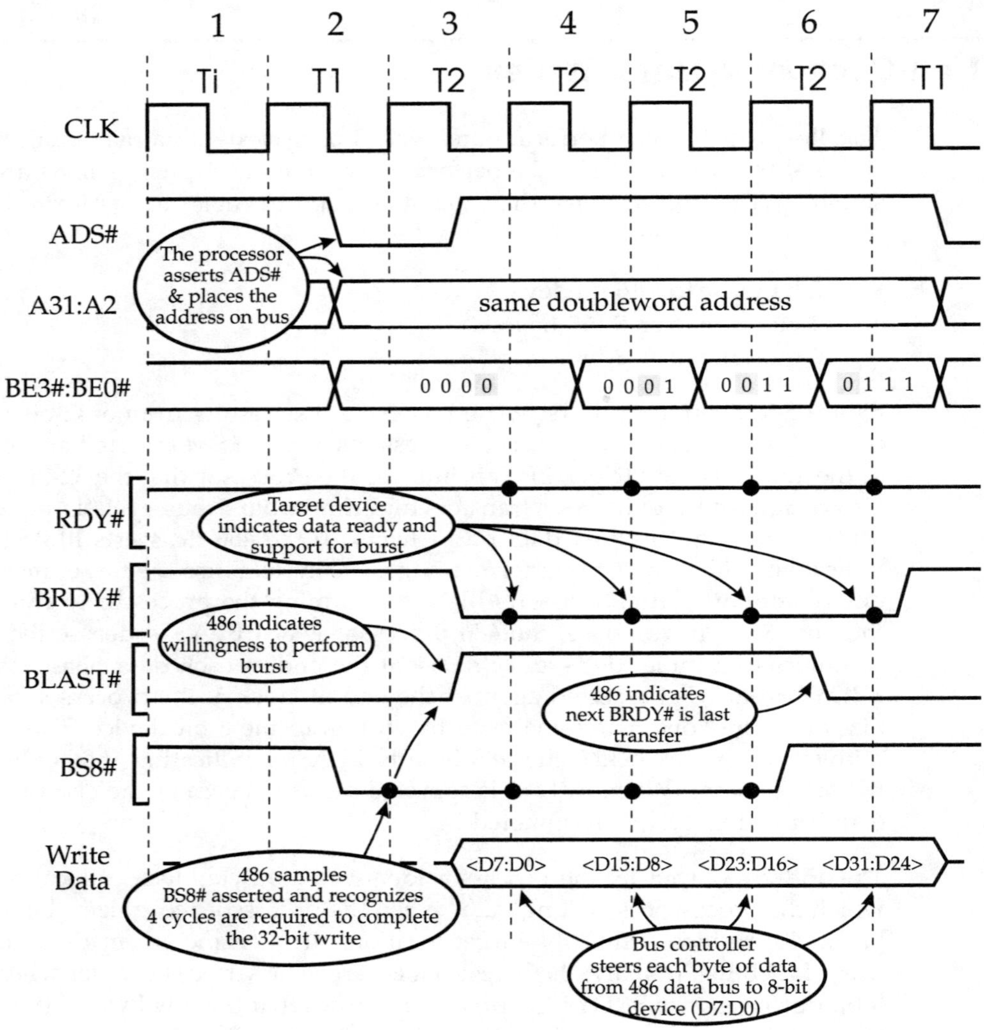

Figure 5-5. Non-Cacheable Burst Write Bus Cycle

Note that the processor outputs the entire 32-bits of data onto the data bus during clock 3 and continues to drive data until the bus cycle completes. External logic (typically the expansion bus controller) is responsible for translating the address to a form recognized by smaller devices and for steering data to the appropriate data paths.

Locked Transfers

Software generates Locked transfers for any instruction that performs a read-modify-write operation. During a read-modify-write operation, the processor can read and modify a variable in external memory and be assured that the variable is not accessed by another bus master between the read and the write.

Locked transfers are generated automatically during certain bus transfers:

- The XCHG (Exchange) instruction generates a locked cycle when one of its operands is memory-based.
- Locked transfers are generated when a segment descriptor is read from memory and then updated.
- Locked transfers are generated when a page directory or page table entry is updated.
- Locked transfers are generated between the two interrupt acknowledge bus cycles that are generated in response to an external hardware interrupt request.

Locked transfers are also generated when the programmer prefixes certain instructions with the LOCK prefix.

When a locked transfer is in progress, the 80486 asserts its LOCK# output. This informs external logic that the external bus structure is owned by the 80486 and should not be granted to another bus master until the locked transfer is completed. LOCK# goes active when the first address and bus cycle definition are output and remains active until RDY# is returned for the last bus cycle.

While LOCK# is active, the 80486 will honor AHOLD and BOFF#, but will not honor HOLD.

Pseudo-Locked Transfers

Pseudo-locked transfers assure that no other bus master will be given control of the external bus structure during operand transfers that take more than one bus cycle. Examples include:

- 8-byte floating-point writes
- 8-byte segment descriptor reads
- Cache line fills

During pseudo-locked transfers, the 80486 asserts the PLOCK# pin. The memory operands must be aligned for proper operation of a pseudo-locked transfer.

Transactions and BOFF# (Bus Cycle Restart)

In some cases, logic external to the 80486 may determine after the microprocessor initiates a memory read bus cycle that the microprocessor will receive stale data from memory if allowed to complete the bus cycle.)

As an example, assume that the microprocessor initiates a memory read bus cycle and that the bus is being snooped by another processor's write-back cache controller. Assume also that the write-back cache has a copy of the memory location's contents and that the cache copy has already been updated by a previous memory write generated by the cache's associated bus master. When the memory write occurred, the cache updated its contents and marked the line as "dirty", but did not generate a memory write to update main memory. This means that the microprocessor is now about to read "stale" data from memory. When the write-back cache detects the snoop hit and the that the line is dirty, it must somehow force the microprocessor to immediately abort the memory read bus cycle so it can perform a memory write to update the memory location with the fresh data.

Bus backoff, BOFF#, is used by the write-back cache to force the 80486 to abort the bus cycle in progress. The BOFF# signal indicates that another bus master needs to complete a bus cycle in order for the microprocessor's current bus cycle to complete successfully.

The microprocessor's response to bus backoff is similar to the bus hold operation, but more immediate; the microprocessor releases the buses in the next clock and no acknowledgment is given. The write-back cache may then seize the bus and perform the memory write to write the fresh data into memory. The write-back cache then removes BOFF#. When BOFF# is deasserted, the processor will immediately restart the same memory read bus cycle that was aborted. The microprocessor then receives fresh data from memory.

Bus backoff is also referred to as bus cycle restart because the aborted bus cycle is restarted when BOFF# is de-asserted. The restarted bus cycle will begin with a new assertion of ADS#, but the transfer will continue from its state when BOFF# was asserted. Any transfers already completed before BOFF# was asserted will be assumed correct and will not be repeated.

The Bus Cycle State Machine

The 80486 bus unit is a state machine possessing five states as defined below. Transitions that occur between the states are illustrated in figure 5-6, and conditions that cause each transition are referenced in table 5-3.

Ti **Bus is idle**. During the idle state address and control outputs may be driven to undefined states, or the bus may be in the high-impedance state (disconnected).

T1 **Address Time**. This state is the first clock of every bus cycle. Valid address and control outputs are driven onto the bus and ADS# is asserted.

T2 **Data Time**. This is the second and subsequent clocks of a bus cycle. Data is driven out (if the cycle is a write), or data is expected (if the cycle is a read), and RDY# and BRDY# pins are sampled.

Tb **Back Off State**. The Bus Unit remains in the Tb state as long as the BOFF# input is active. During this period, the microprocessor remains disconnected from the buses.

T1b **Restart after back off**. This state is the first clock of a restarted bus cycle. Valid address and control outputs are driven out and ADS# is asserted. This state cannot be distinguished from T1 externally.

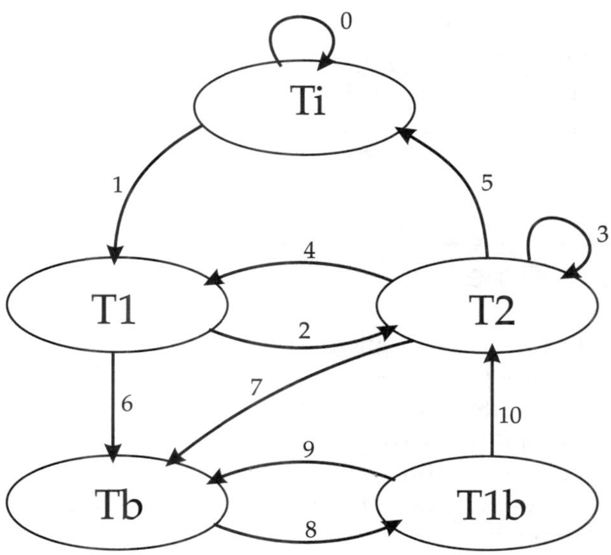

Figure 5-6. 80486 Bus Cycle States

Table 5-3. Definition of State Transitions Illustrated in Figure 5-6

Ref #	State Transition Description
0	No bus request is pending
1	The 486 processor starts a bus cycle by driving the address and bus cycle definition onto the buses. Occurs only when HOLD, AHOLD, and BOFF# are deasserted.
2	The processor always proceeds from T1 to T2 unless BOFF# is asserted. In this case the processor suspends the bus cycle until BOFF# is released.
3	The processor always stays in T2 (adding wait states) until RDY# or the last BRDY# is asserted, or unless BOFF# is asserted.
4	The processor returns to T1 when the current bus cycle ends if another bus cycle is pending. Occurs only when HOLD, AHOLD, and BOFF# are deasserted.
5	The processor transitions from T2 to Ti after the bus cycle ends, if no other bus cycle is pending.
6	When in state T1, if BOFF# is asserted the processor aborts the bus cycle and transitions to Tb. The bus unit stays in Tb until BOFF# is deasserted.
7	The bus unit transitions from T2 to Tb when BOFF# is asserted.
8	When BOFF# is released, the bus unit restarts the bus cycle by driving the address and bus cycle definition onto the buses. If BOFF# occurs during a burst the processor retains data acquired prior to the BOFF# and completes the bus cycle from the point of suspension.
9	The processor returns to Tb from T1b if BOFF# is asserted again.
10	The processor always proceeds from T1b to T2 unless BOFF# is asserted.

I/O Recovery Time

Many I/O devices will malfunction if two, back-to-back I/O writes to the same device are performed too closely together. The I/O device requires a recovery period after the first write in order to ensure that it captures the data from the second I/O write correctly. This is known as the I/O recovery time. I/O device recovery time must be handled differently by the 80486 than the 80386. I/O device back-to-back write recovery times could be guaranteed by the 80386 microprocessor by inserting a jump to the next instruction in between the two OUT instructions that write to the device. The jump forces the 80386 microprocessor to flush its Prefetch Queue and generate a Prefetch bus cycle to fetch the second OUT instruction from memory again. The delay imposed by the memory read to fetch the second OUT instruction again acts as a buffer period between the two I/O writes.

Inserting a jump to the next instruction will not work with the 80486 microprocessor because the prefetch could be satisfied by the on-chip cache. One solution suggested by Intel follows:

> *A read cycle must be explicitly generated to a non-cacheable location in memory to guarantee that a read bus cycle is performed. This memory read will not be allowed to propagate to the external buses until after the I/O write has completed because I/O writes are not buffered. The time that elapses during the non-cacheable memory read bus cycle will give the I/O device time to recover before the next I/O write begins on the external buses.*

Since the location of a non-cacheable memory location is a platform configuration-specific characteristic, a program using this methodology might fail with some platform configurations. A more universal solution would be to perform an I/O read from an I/O location that will not be affected by the read (in a PC-compatible environment, I/O address 61h would serve). This will force the microprocessor to perform an I/O read bus cycle in between the two I/O writes, thereby guaranteeing at least two PCLK cycles of delay between the two I/O writes to the target device.

Write Buffers

General

The 80486 microprocessor contains four write buffers to enhance the performance of consecutive writes to memory. The buffers can be filled at the rate of one write per clock until all four buffers are filled.

When all four buffers are empty and the external buses are idle, a write request will propagate directly to the external buses, bypassing the write buffers. If the buses are not available at the time the write request is generated internally, the write will be placed in the write buffers and will be propagated to the external buses as soon the buses become available. If the write is a write hit in the internal cache, however, the write data will be stored in the internal cache immediately. Writes will be driven onto the external buses in the same order they were placed in the write buffers.

Under certain conditions, a memory read will be routed to the external buses in front of the writes currently pending in the write buffers (even though the writes occurred earlier in the program execution).

A memory read will be reordered in front of all writes in the write buffers under the following conditions:

- all writes pending in the buffers are cache hits
- the read is a cache miss

Following these rules, the 80486 will not attempt to read from an external memory location that needs to be updated by one of the pending writes.

Reordering of a read before the pending writes can only be done once, after which all the write buffers are flushed prior to the next memory read.

The Write Buffers and I/O Cycles

I/O cycles must be handled differently by the write buffer logic. I/O reads are never ordered in front of memory writes. This ensures that the 80486 will update all memory locations prior to checking the status of an I/O device.

The 80486 microprocessor never buffers single I/O writes. When processing an OUT instruction, internal execution stops until the I/O write actually completes on the external buses. This allows time for external logic to drive a cache invalidation cycle into the 80486 or to mask interrupts before the microprocessor progresses to the next instruction. Repeated OUTS instructions will be buffered.

Chapter 6

The Previous Chapter

The previous chapter summarized and defined the bus transactions that can be run by the 80486 microprocessor. The chapter focused on single transfer bus cycles, dynamic bus sizing, and non-cache burst bus cycles.

This Chapter

This chapter discusses the SL technology features implemented in the 486DX family of processors. Focus is placed on System Management Mode (SMM) and clock control.

The Next Chapter

The next chapter discusses the changes to the 486 microprocessor's software environment from that of the 80386 microprocessor.

Introduction to SL Technology Used in the 486 Processors

The term "SL technology" originated with the introduction of the Intel 386SL products. The SL processors were highly integrated and incorporated items such as the memory controller, ISA bus controller, and numerous power management features. The major SL power management features are now incorporated into nearly all of Intel's processors. However, early versions of the 486DX and 486SX processors did not incorporate Intel's SL technology features. Current versions of these processors, as well as the rest of the 486 family of products (except the 50MHz 486DX) now incorporate the SL technology features. The SL technology implemented in the 486 processors includes:

- System Management Mode (SMM) operation — SMM provides an operational mode that permits power management code to execute in a way that is transparent to the operating system and application programs.
- Stop Clock (STPCLK#) capability — the STPCLK# input provides the system designer with the ability to stop the processor core and remove its clock input, resulting in a tremendous reduction in processor power consumption.
- Auto-HALT power down — processors implementing this feature automatically enter a low power state when the processor enters the HALT state (i.e. executes a HALT instruction).
- 3.3vdc operation — the lower operating voltage also reduces the power consumed by the processor. Note that some 486 processors operate at 5vdc, but still implement the other SL technology features.

System Management Mode (SMM)

System management mode (SMM) simplifies system design when implementing control features such as power management. Early implementations of these features were not typically transparent to the operating system and application programs. As a result, power management implementations required customized software drivers and operating systems. SMM eliminates this requirement because code used to perform power management is executes from a completely separate address space, which is transparent to other system software (See figure 6-1).

A common implementation of power management is to turn power off to a device when it has been idle for a specified amount of time. The next access to the device will fail since it has been powered off. Power management hardware detects the attempted access, causing power management software to be called. The software reapplies power to the device and ensures that the I/O instruction that attempted the access is re-executed.

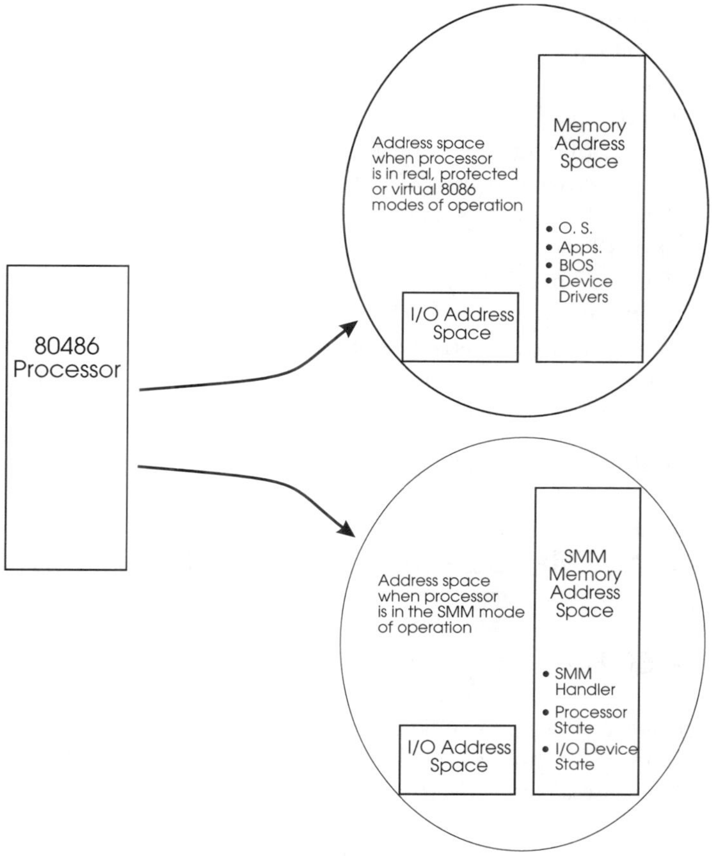

Figure 6-1. Address Space Available to Processor when Operating in Different Modes

Power management events (e.g. a request to power down an inactive device) cause system management mode (SMM) to be invoked via the system management interrupt (SMI#) pin. The following steps introduce the actions taken by the processor when SMI# is asserted.

- The processor recognizes SMI# and asserts SMI acknowledge (SMIACT#).
- SMIACT# notifies the system that the next processor access will be to system management memory (SMRAM). This causes the system to enable access to SMRAM and disable access to normal system RAM.
- Current processor state information (internal registers) is saved to SMRAM via a series of memory writes.

- The processor enters SMM after setting internal registers to their initial SMM state.
- The processor jumps to the entry point in SMRAM where the SMI handler resides.
- Power management status registers are checked by the SMI handler to determine what initiated the SMI request.
- The SMI handler services the power management request (e.g. saving the state of the inactive device to SMRAM and powering it down).
- The SMI handler upon completing its task issues the return from system-management mode (RSM) instruction.
- The processor retrieves and restores the saved processor state from SMRAM and continues normal program execution from main DRAM memory.

The following sections detail these steps.

System Management Memory (SMRAM)

The SMRAM Address Map

Figure 6-2 illustrates a typical layout for SMRAM. The processor pre-defines the range of addresses within SMRAM that are used to save the processor's state (context) when entering SMM. The processor also specifies the entry point of the SMI code. These locations are relative to the base address of the SMRAM. The other areas of SMRAM illustrated in figure 6-2 are implementation specific and left up to the SMM programmer to define.

The base address of SMRAM is set by the processor to a default value of 30000h. The processor defines a 512 byte region of SMRAM starting at location 3FFFFh (SMRAM base + FFFFh) downward to 3FE00h for saving the processor's context. Once the processor's context is saved, the processor jumps to the entry point of the SMI handler at SMM location 38000h (SMRAM base + 8000h). The SMI handler then executes its routine within SMRAM, using it to store data and stacks as required.

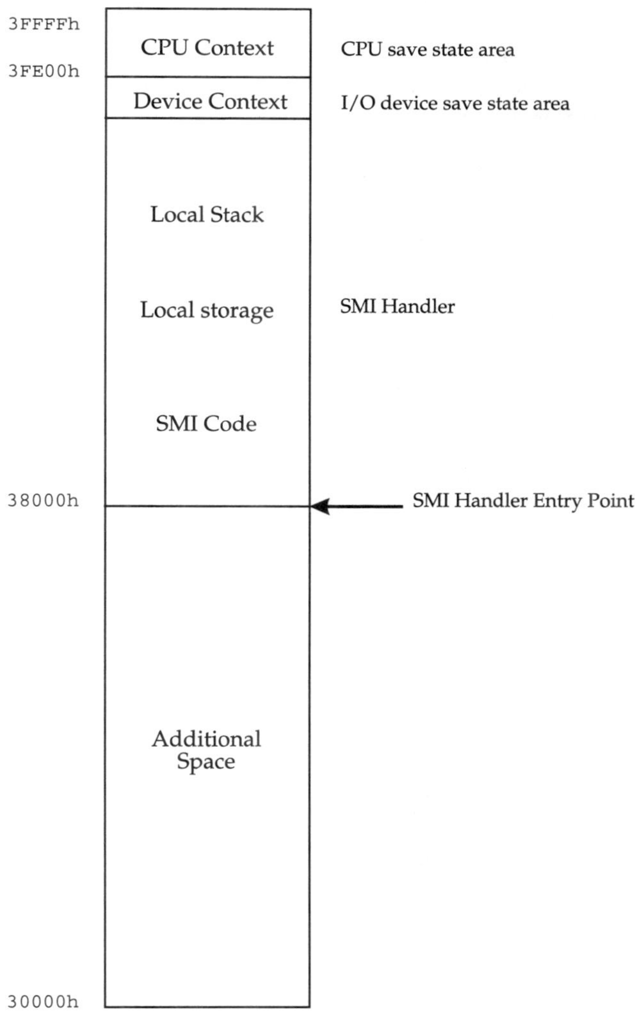

Figure 6-2. Sample Layout of SMM Memory

Figure 6-3 contrasts the processor's address space when SMM is disabled and when it's enabled. SMRAM is shown residing at its default location in SMM address space. The minimum amount of SMRAM that can be implemented must be large enough to hold the SMI# handler and the area used to store the processor's state. This 32KB region begins at the SMI handler entry point (SMRAM base + 8000h (38000h by default)) and ends at the top of the state save area (SMRAM base + FFFFh (3FFFFh by default)). Note that when the processor enters SMM, SMRAM overlays a region of physical memory that is normally accessible when not in SMM. All other physical memory that is accessible to the programmer during normal operation is also available to the SMI handler during SMM.

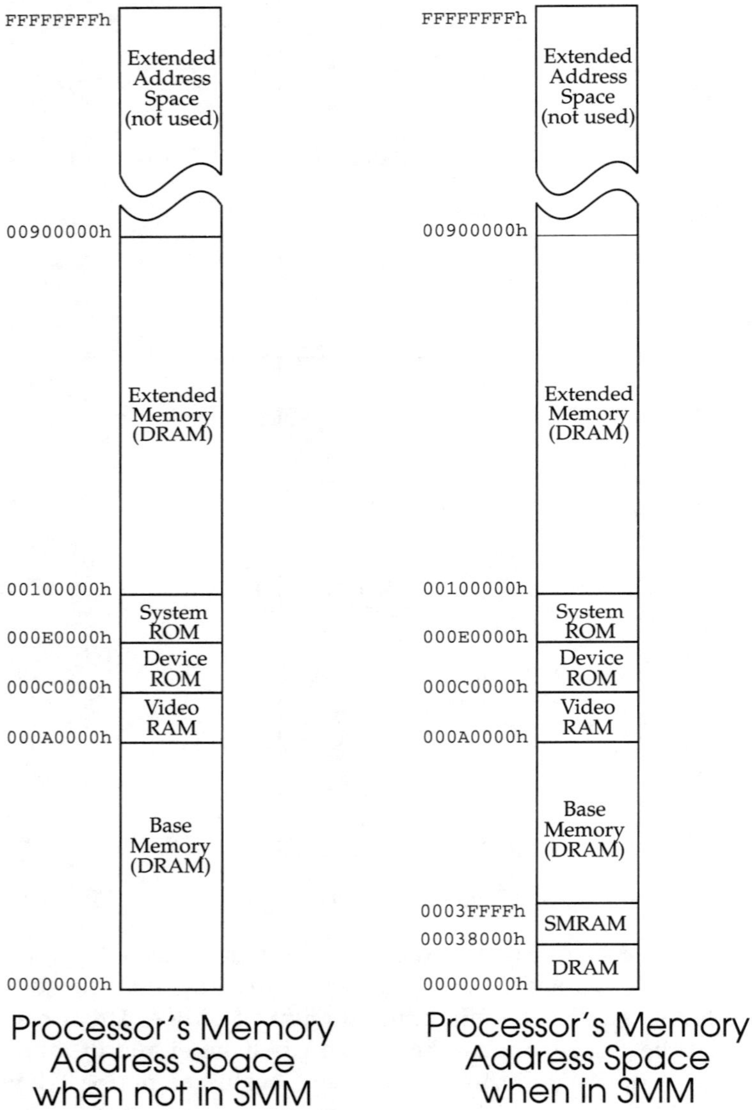

Figure 6-3. Typical PC Memory Map (SMM Disabled versus SMM Enabled)

Initializing SMRAM

Before the first SMI request is issued, the POST programmer must initialize SMM by loading the SMI handler into SMRAM. The SMRAM is normally accessible only when the processor is servicing an SMI request. However, the system must permit remapping SMRAM into the processor's real address space to allow the POST programmer to load the SMI handler into SMRAM, prior to the processor entering SMM. Once the SMM code (SMI handler) is loaded into SMRAM, the system is ready to handle SMI requests and SMRAM is mapped back into SMM address space.

Changing the SMRAM Base Address

When the processor RESETs, the SMRAM base address defaults to 30000h. Therefore, when entering SMM for the first time, SMRAM will be mapped to the default address. The SMI handler however, can relocate the SMRAM by changing the SMBASE Relocation slot in the processor's state save area. (See figure 6-4.) SMRAM can be relocated to any 32KB aligned location within the 4GB of SMM address space. (See also the section entitled, "SMBASE Slot.")

Entering SMM

The System Asserts SMI

All system management requests are issued to the processor via the SMI# signal. SMI# is a falling-edge #sensitive interrupt. To guarantee that SMI# is recognized at the instruction boundary of an instruction that causes the SMI# to be invoked, (e.g. an instruction that accesses an I/O device that is powered down), SMI# must be asserted at least three clocks before BRDY# is returned. When the processor recognizes SMI# asserted, it enters SMM mode if the SMI is the highest priority interrupt request currently pending execution. Interrupt request pins having higher priority than SMI# include:

- RESET/SRESET
- FLUSH#

These interrupt requests will be serviced by the processor prior to acknowledging the SMI#. However, if FLUSH# and SMI# are both asserted, the SMI#

is latched by the processor and serviced when its priority comes up (i.e. after the FLUSH# is serviced). The SMI# must be asserted for at least one clock cycle to be recognized, and must remain deasserted for at least four clock cycles before it is guaranteed to be recognized again.

Back-to-Back SMI Requests

After an SMI request is recognized, the SMI# pin is masked by the processor until the end of the SMI service routine (i.e. RSM is executed). If another SMI request is asserted while a current SMI is being serviced, it is latched and will be serviced when the current SMI completes. The second SMI request is recognized on the instruction boundary caused by the RSM instruction. As a result, back-to-back SMIs are run without returning to the program that was interrupted. Note that the processor can only latch a single SMI request at a time. In the previous example, if a third SMI request was asserted it would be lost.

SMI and Cache Coherency

As illustrated in figure 6-3, the default SMRAM address space overlaps a portion of main DRAM. The internal caches might have copies of the DRAM locations that SMRAM will overlay when the processor enters SMM. When the processor enters SMM, access to any of these cached locations results in cache incoherency. To prevent this from occurring the system designer must ensure that the caches are flushed prior to entering SMM. This can be accomplished by asserting the FLUSH# pin along with SMI#. Since FLUSH# has a higher priority than SMI#, the internal caches will be flushed before the processor enters SMM. External caches must also be flushed in the same manner.

If normal memory and SMRAM do not overlap, then flushing the cache upon entry to SMM is not necessary. Similarly, if normal memory is not cacheable, then the caches do not require flushing.

See the section entitled, "Exiting SMM" regarding cache coherency when SMRAM is cacheable.

Pending Writes are Flushed to System Memory

Once the processor has entered SMM, some system memory may be hidden by SMRAM if it overlays a portion of normal memory. Therefore, after SMI# is recognized by the processor and before it asserts SMIACT#, it completes all transfers to external memory including all buffered write operations. This eliminates the possibility of data in the write buffers being written to SMRAM and not normal memory.

SMIACT# is Asserted (SMRAM Accessed)

The processor asserts the SMIACT# signal to notify the memory controller that the processor is entering SMM. If SMRAM overlays some portion of system memory, then the memory controller must disable the normal system memory address range that SMRAM overlays. When SMIACT# is asserted system logic disables the portion of normal memory that SMRAM overlays and enables SMRAM.

Processor Saves Its State

The first action taken by the processor when entering SMM is to save the current state, or context, of the processor. All registers listed in figure 6-4 are written to SMRAM in a stack-like fashion from the top of the state save address location downward. The offsets shown in figure 6-4 are relative to the SMI entry point.

Note that some of the locations within the state-save map can be written to by the SMI handler. When the processor exits SMM the state-save information is restored to the processor's registers, thereby loading the changed values.

Four entries within the state-save map are specific to SMM:

- Auto-HALT Restart slot
- SMM Revision Identifier slot
- SMBASE Slot
- I/O instruction restart slot

Offset from SMI Entry Point	Bits 31 ... 16	Bits 15 ... 0
7FFC	CR0	
7FF8	CR3	
7FF4	EFLAGS*	
7FF0	EIP*	
7FEC	EDI*	
7FE8	ESI*	
7FE4	EBP*	
7FE0	ESP*	
7FDC	EBX*	
7FD8	EDX*	
7FD4	ECX*	
7FD0	EAX*	
7FCC	DR6	
7FC8	DR7	
7FC4	Reserved	TR
7FC0	Reserved	LDT Base
7FBC	Reserved	GS
7FB8	Reserved	FS
7FB4	Reserved	DS
7FB0	Reserved	SS
7FAC	Reserved	CS
7FA8	Reserved	ES
7FA7-7F98	Reserved	
7F94	IDT Base	
7F93-7F8C	Reserved	
7F88	GDT Base	
7F87-7F04	Reserved	
7F00	Auto HALT Restart Slot*	I/O Instruc. Restart*
7EFC	SMM Revision Identifier	
7EF8	SMBASE Slot*	
7EF7-7E00	Reserved	

31 · · · · · · · · · · · Bits · · · · · · · · · · · 0

*Locations are writable

Figure 6-4. The Processor's SMM State-Save Map

Auto-HALT Restart

This slot in the state-save map indicates whether the processor was in the HALT state when entering SMM. Bit 0 is the only bit defined within the Auto-HALT Restart slot and is set as follow:

- If the processor was not in the HALT state when it entered SMM, then bit 0 is reset to 0. When this value is restored, the processor returns to the next sequential instruction. Setting bit 0 to a 1 causes unpredictable behavior.
- If the processor was in the HALT state when the SMI# pin was asserted, then bit 0 is set to 1. When this value is restored, the processor returns to the HALT state and performs a HALT special cycle. The SMI handler can change bit 0 to a 1 causing the processor to return to the next instruction following the HALT instruction.

SMM Revision Identifier

The SMM revision identifier is read-only and indicates the SMM version and extensions supported by this processor. Figure 6-5 illustrates the contents of the revision identifier.

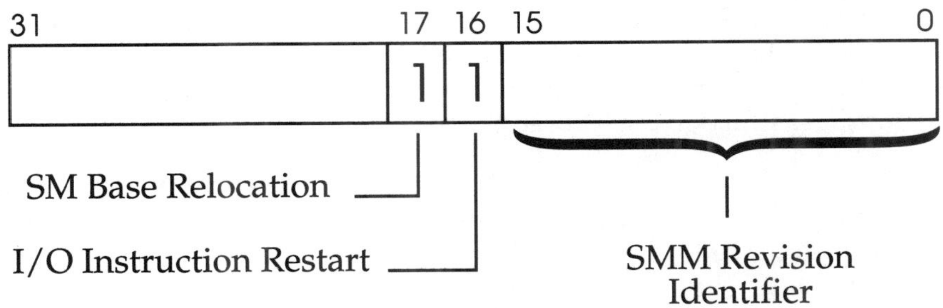

Figure 6-5. SMM Revision Identifier Definition

The lower sixteen bits define the revision level of the SMM architecture. The upper sixteen bits are used for indicating support for available extensions.

- I/O Instruction Restart (bit 16=0) — indicates that the processor supports this feature.
- SM Base Relocation (bit 17=1) — indicates support for relocating the SMRAM base address in memory.

SMBASE

This slot identifies the starting address of SMRAM as specified by bit 17 of the SMM revision identifier. The SMRAM base address defaults to 30000h when the processor RESETs. However, the SMI handler can move the SMRAM base address to any 32KB aligned location within the 4GB of SMM address space. This is accomplished by writing the new address into the SMBASE slot in the state-save area. Note that the SMI handler must relocate its code to the new entry point before exiting SMM. When the processor executes the RSM instruction and restores the state-save map, the new SMBASE address takes effect. The next time SMI# is asserted the processor calculates the new SMI entry point and the location of the state-save map as follows:

- SMI Entry Point = SMRAM base + 8000h
- State-Save location = SMRAM base + [8000h + 7FFFh]

I/O Instruction Restart

In many instances, the SMI# pins is asserted by external hardware when an access occurs to an I/O device that is powered down. When the SMI handler is called, it re-applies power to the target device and returns to the interrupt program. Since the I/O instruction that caused the SMI has not actually written to the target device, it must be executed again. The 486 processors support the I/O instruction restart feature, that instructs the processor to restart the I/O instruction that caused the SMI to occur.

The I/O instruction restart slot in the state save map permits the SMI handler to inform the processor to restart the instruction that completed execution when the SMI# was recognized. Thus, when the RSM instruction is executed, the state save map is restored, and the processor re-executes the I/O instruction. This time the instruction has its intended effect since the SMI handler has re-applied power to the target device.

When the processor saves it state, the value of the I/O restart slot is always 0000h. The SMI handler, recognizing that the SMI was triggered by an access to a device that is powered down, re-applies power and writes 00FFh to the I/O instruction restart slot. When the processor restores the state-save map the new I/O instruction restart slot value of 00FFh causes the processor to execute the I/O instruction again.

In order for I/O instruction restart to work correctly, the SMI# signal must be recognized on the instruction boundary of the I/O instruction causing the SMI. To meet the setup time for recognizing SMI# on an instruction boundary,

SMI# must be asserted at least 3 PCLKs prior to BRDY# being sampled asserted.

When an SMI that is currently executing sets the I/O instruction restart slot and a second SMI is asserted, the processor services the second SMI before restarting the I/O instruction. Note that two back-to-back SMI sequences that both specify I/O instruction restart will be handled incorrectly. Therefore, the SMI handler must not set the I/O instruction restart slot during the second of two consecutive SMIs. A second consecutive I/O instruction restart causes the EIP to be decremented a second time, and therefore, no longer points to the I/O instruction.

The Processor Enters SMM

When the SMI# pin is asserted the processor may be executing code in any one of the processor's other modes of operation: Real mode, VM86 mode, or protected mode. Once the processor saves its current state to SMRAM, it initializes its internal registers in preparation for entering SMM mode. Table 6-1 shows the initial core register contents upon entry to SMM.

Table 6-1. Initial Core Register Values for SMM

Register Name	Contents
General Purpose Registers	Unpredictable
EFLAGS	00000002h
EIP	00008000h
CS Selector	3000h
CS Base	00030000h (default)
DS, ES, FS, GS, SS Selectors	0000h
DS, ES, FS, GS, SS Bases	00000000h
DS, ES, FS, GS, SS Limits	FFFFFFFFh
CR0	Bits 0,2,3 & 31 cleared (PE, EM, TS & PG); others are unchanged
DR6	unpredictable
DR7	00000000h

The operating conditions of the processor based on these values are as follows:

- CR0, bit 0 (protected mode enable) is cleared, therefore the processor uses real mode address calculation.
- CS:IP values result in the SMI entry point of 38000h.
- All segment and limit values (except CS) define a 4GB segment (i.e. the segment base address of 00000000h and the limit of FFFFFFFFh creates a single 4GB segment).
- CR0, bit 2 (EM) is cleared so that no floating-point exceptions are generated.
- CR0, bit 3 (task switch) and 31 (paging enable) are cleared, since SMM does not operate in protected mode.
- CR0, bit 8 (trap or single-step flag) is cleared disabling the single-step exception.
- CR0, bit 9 (interrupt enable) is cleared, disabling the processor's INTR input.
- DR7 is cleared to disable debug traps. (Except bits 12 and 13)

When in SMM, the processor uses real mode addressing, however some aspects of the processor's operation differs from standard real mode operation. The following sections highlight the processor's capabilities when in SMM.

Address Space

When in SMM mode, the processor is capable of accessing all I/O address space and can access the entire 4GB of memory address space. The ability to access the entire 4GB of address space must be accomplished with 32-bit offsets within a segment whose start address must be within the first 1MB of address space, since real-mode style addressing is used.

Exceptions and Interrupts

Upon entry to SMM the processor blocks NMIs and disables INTRs. These interrupts are disabled because the interrupt service routines are not aware of the existence of SMRAM. If the SMRAM overlays a portion of the interrupt service routine itself or any memory location accessed by the routine, the results would be unpredictable but devastating. For the same reason, debug and single-step traps are also disabled. An SMM programmer wishing to service maskable interrupts or use these traps within SMM may re-enable them, but must ensure that the routines called do not conflict with SMRAM. Note that software interrupts are permitted in SMM, however, the same potential conflicts and solutions apply. It is the responsibility of the SMI handler to ensure no conflicts occur.

Executing the SMI Handler

Once the processor has initialized itself, it enters SMM and jumps to the entry point where the SMI handler resides. The SMI handler first checks status registers to determine the nature of the SMI request. Once the request is identified, the handler then executes the specified management routine to handle the request. The SMI handler may be designed to handle a wide variety of requests. Typical requests might include:

- Saving the state of a device
- Powering down an idle device
- Powering up a device that has been accessed
- Stopping or slowing down oscillators and clocks
- Saving state information for entire system (to non-volatile memory) and powering the system down
- Managing security protection

When the SMI handler completes its task, it executes the Return from System Management mode (RSM) instruction, thereby returning the processor to normal program flow.

Exiting SMM

The processor exits SMM by executing the RSM instruction. The RSM instruction is only valid when in SMM mode. Any attempt to execute this instruction in any other modes results in an invalid op-code error.

Processor's Response to RSM

The RSM instruction causes the processor to flush all write buffers and then to restore the state-save map. This returns the processor to the same exact state (except for the control slots) that it was in prior to the system management interrupt request. Next the processor deasserts the SMIACT# signal and the interrupted program can continue execution.

State Save Area Restored

Three control slots implemented within the state-save map allow modifications to the information restored to the processor. These are the:

- **Auto HALT Restart control slot**. This slot gives the SMM handler the ability to specify how the processor should exit SMM if the processor was halted upon entry to SMM. The default condition is to return the processor to the HALT state when exiting SMM. In this case, the processor performs a halt special cycle to notify external logic that it is entering the HALT state. This default action occurs if the Auto HALT Restart control slot is not modified by the SMI handler. If the control slot is reset to zero, the processor returns to the instruction following the HALT instruction, permitting program execution to continue.
- **I/O instruction restart control slot**. The slot directs the processor to re-execute the instruction that just completed when the SMI# pin was recognized by the instruction, causing entry into SMM. This permits the processor to re-execute an I/O instruction that attempted to access a device that was powered down, thereby causing the SMI. Once the SMI handler has re-applied power to the device, it can write 00FFh to the I/O instruction restart slot, and upon return from SMM the processor will execute the I/O instruction again.
- **SMBASE relocation slot**. The SMI handler may also change the SMRAM base address, causing the processor to vector to a new SMI handler entry point the next time an SMI request is serviced.

If the processor recognizes that invalid information is restored from the state-save map, it enters the SHUTDOWN state and the processor performs a shutdown special cycle. This occurs when:

- the SMBASE slot contains a value that is not 32KB aligned.
- a reserved bit of CR4 is set to 1.
- CR0 contains an illegal bit combination.

Maintaining Cache Coherency When SMRAM is Cacheable

If SMRAM is cacheable and it overlays normal DRAM memory that is also cacheable, the syste must ensure that the caches are flushed prior to returning to normal mode. This can be accomplished by causing the FLUSH# pin to be asserted when SMIACT# is deasserted. FLUSH# must be asserted within one clock of SMIACT # being deasserted.

If SMRAM is not cacheable or if cacheable but does not overlay cacheable memory, then no cache coherency problems will result.

486 Clock Control

The 486 implements four states that interact to provide the processor with a variety of methods for slowing or stopping the clock, thereby conserving power. The clock control states are:

- Stop Grant state
- Stop Clock state
- Auto HALT Power Down state
- Stop Clock Snoop State

Figure 6-6 illustrates the stop clock state machine. The normal state represents the processor running normally at full clock frequency. The following sections describe each of the clock control states.

The Stop Grant State

The 486 processors provide a STPCLK# pin that directs the processor to stop its internal clock. All Intel 486 processors that have a X1 clock input implement an internal PLL (phase-lock loop). The clock input to the PLL remains active, but the PLL output is stopped, thereby removing the clock from the processor core. This is known as the "Stop Grant" state.

The STPCLK# signal is implemented as the lowest priority interrupt input to the processor. This ensures that all other forms of interrupt request are handled prior to stopping the processor's internal clock. The processor checks interrupt inputs after completing execution of each instruction. If STPCLK# is the only interrupt pending execution, the processor immediately stops execution and takes the following actions:

- stops the prefetch unit
- flushes the instruction pipeline
- completes all pending (buffered) writes
- performs a "stop grant" special cycle
- waits for RDY# or BRDY# to be asserted and stops the internal clock (enters the "stop grant" state)

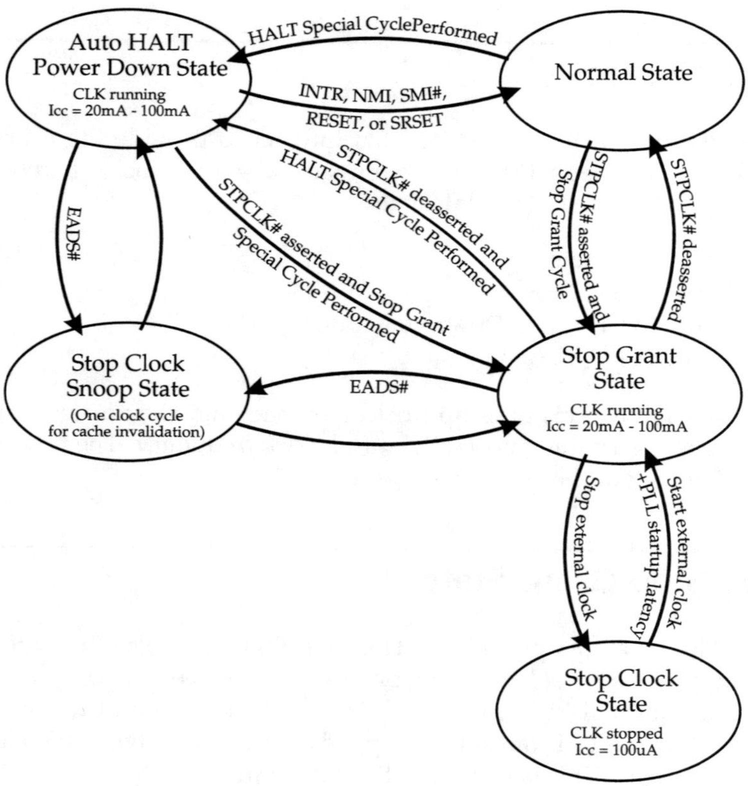

Figure 6-6. Stop Clock State Diagram

Note that the processor cannot enter the stop grant state while HLDA is asserted (because the stop grant special cycle cannot be performed).

The stop grant special cycle is performed when the processor outputs the signals shown in table 6-2. Following the stop grant special cycle, the processor stops its internal clock and enters the stop grant state.

Table 6-2. Stop Grant Special Cycle Definition

Signal(s)	Signal State(s)
M/IO#	0b
D/C#	0b
W/R#	1b
A31:A2	00000010h
BE3#:BE0#	1011b

The processor restarts it internal clock and returns to the interrupted application when STPCLK# is deasserted (driven high, not floated).

Stop Clock State

Once the processor has entered the Stop Grant state, it will transition to the stop clock state if external logic removes the clock signal from the processor. This is the lowest power consumption state that the processor can operate in. The processor returns to the Stop Grant state after the clock has been restored to the CLK input and held at a constant frequency for at least 1ms (PLL startup latency).

When the processor is in the stop clock state, all processor inputs should remain stable (except INTR, NMI, and SMI#). If any other inputs change state, the processor's operation will be unpredictable when it returns to the stop grant state.

Auto-HALT Power Down

The 486 microprocessor automatically stops the clock to its core logic when it enters the HALT state. This occurs when the processor executes a HALT instruction. The processor first executes a HALT special bus cycle and then stops the internal clock to conserve power. When the processor exits the HALT state, due to an NMI, INTR, or SMI#, it restores the clock to the core logic and the processor continues normal operation. The processor also returns to the normal state when RESET or SRESET is asserted.

Note that the processor also responds to the STPCLK# signal when in the Auto-HALT Power Down state. In response to STPCLK# assertion, the processor performs a stop grant special cycle and transitions to the Stop Grant state. The processor will transition back to the Auto HALT Power Down state if STPCLK# is deasserted and the processor has not recovered from HALT (i.e. no NMI, INTR, or SMI#). The processor will perform a HALT special cycle to notify external logic of the state change.

Stop Clock Snoop State

When the processor is in either the Stop Grant or Auto HALT Power Down state the processor continues to recognize valid cache snoop operations. A snoop, or cache invalidation cycle, can occur once the system has asserted either HOLD, AHOLD, or BOFF#. The processor then monitors EADS# to detect when an cache invalidation cycle should be performed. When EADS# is asserted, the processors re-applies the clock to the processor core for one complete clock cycle so the cache directory look-up can be performed. Following the snoop, the clock is once again removed from the processor core and the clock state transitions back to the previous state.

Chapter 7

The Previous Chapter

The previous chapter introduced and detailed the SL technology features implemented into later models of the 486DX and other 486 family products. The chapter focused on system management mode operation and the stop clock features.

This Chapter

This chapter discusses the changes to the x86 software environment introduced and implemented in the latest 486DX processors.

The Next Chapter

The next chapter details the differences between the 486SX processors and the 486DX processors.

Changes to the Software Environment

This chapter summarizes the registers implemented within the 486 microprocessor and details the changes to the software environment. These changes include:

- Instruction set enhancements
- New control register (CR4)
- Additional bits added to status and control registers
- Additional bits defined for memory paging
- New test registers for internal cache
- Floating-point registers integrated into processor

Instruction Set Enhancements

The 80486 is 100% code compatible with the 80386 microprocessor. Seven new instructions have been added to the instruction repertoire:

- **Exchange and Add**. The XADD instruction can be used to optimize parallel loop execution.
- **Compare and Exchange**. The CMPXCHG instruction is intended for use in testing and manipulating software semaphores. When executed, it compares the EAX register to the destination. If they are equal, the source is loaded to the destination. If they are not equal, the destination is loaded to the EAX register. The Zero flag is set if they are equal and cleared if they aren't.
- **Invalidate Cache**. The INVD instruction causes the internal cache to be invalidated (flushed). In addition, the 80486 executes a special bus cycle type to command the external, secondary cache to flush its contents as well.
- **Write Back and Invalidate**. The WBINVD instruction causes the following actions to take place:
  - internal cache is flushed.
  - 80486 executes a special bus cycle type to command the external cache to write all dirty lines back to main memory and flush its contents (if it's a write-back cache).
- **Invalidate TLB Entry**. The INVLPG instruction invalidates a single entry in the Translation Lookaside Buffer (TLB). The programmer specifies a memory location using virtual (paging) addressing. If the specified address has a corresponding entry in the TLB, it will be marked invalid.
- **Return from System Management Mode**. The RSM instruction causes the processor to exit SMM and return to normal mode. The processor takes the following actions when executing an RSM instruction:
  - flushes all write buffers
  - restores the state-save map, returning the processor to its state prior to SMI# being recognized
  - deasserts the SMIACT# signal to re-enable access to normal memory
  - fetches and execute instructions from main memory
- **CPUID.** This instruction reads the contents of the CPUID register and is used to determine the processor type and capabilities.
- **Byte Swap**. The BSWAP instruction reverses the byte order of a 32-bit register. Refer to figure 7-1. When data is transferred between a register and memory by an Intel processor, the order used is always little-endian.

software written for the VAX also uses the little-endian methodology. Since some processor types (e.g., IBM non-PC systems, Motorola 68000 series) stores data in the reverse order (Big-Endian), BSWAP can be used to reorder data to allow efficient access to existing databases built on big-endian machines.

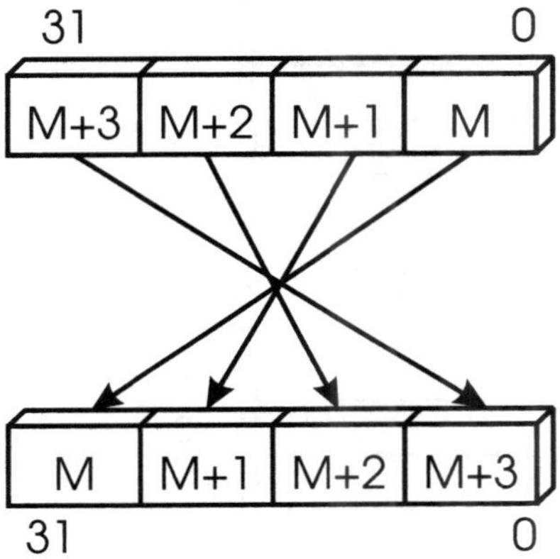

BSWAP (Byte Swap)
- reverses byte order of a 32-bit register
- allows only 32-bit registers
- converts little Endian to Big Endian and vice versa

Figure 7-1. The BSWAP Instruction

The Register Set

Base Architecture Registers

Refer to figure 7-2. The base architecture registers consists of the following register groups:

- General-Purpose Registers
- Segment Registers
- Extended Instruction Pointer (EIP)
- Extended Flags Register (EFLAGS)

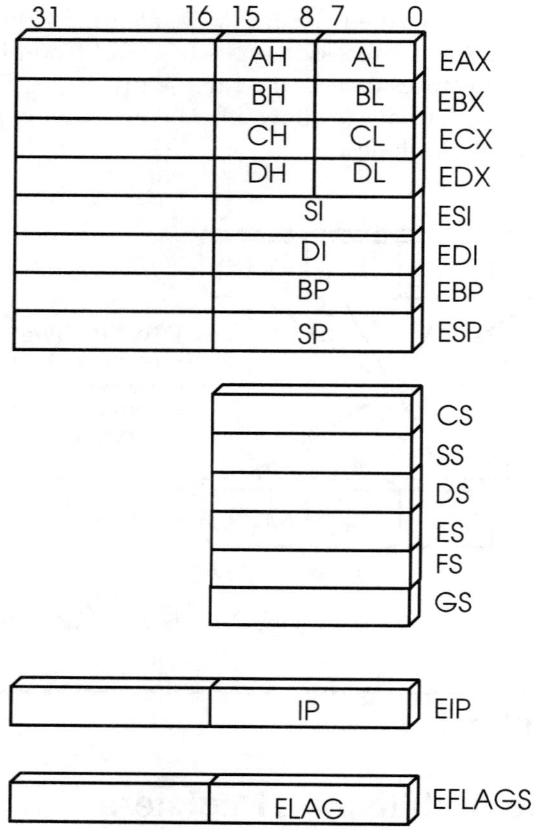

Figure 7-2. 80486 Base Architecture Registers

With the exception of the flags register, all of these registers are 80386-compatible. Figure 7-3 illustrates the definition of the 486 EFlags register. The original 486DX, 486SX, and 486DX2 processors included only the alignment check (AC) bit of those designated as new. The new bits include:

- AC (Alignment Check) — This bit enables generation of a fault condition when a memory reference is made to a misaligned address. A misaligned access is a doubleword access to an address that is not on a doubleword address boundary, or an 8-byte reference to an address that is not on a 64-bit (8 byte) word address boundary.
- VIF (Virtual Interrupt Flag) — This bit is a virtual image of the IF (interrupt enable flag) and is used during execution of virtual 8086 applications. Details of its use are under non-disclosure.

- VIP (Virtual Interrupt Pending flag) — This flag is used in conjunction with the VIF bit to provide support in multitasking environments. Details of its use are also under non-disclosure.
- ID (Identification flag) — This bit provides the programmer with a mechanism for determining it the processor supports the CPUID instructions. If the ID bit can be set and cleared by the programmer, this the processor includes an ID register and supports the CPUID instruction.

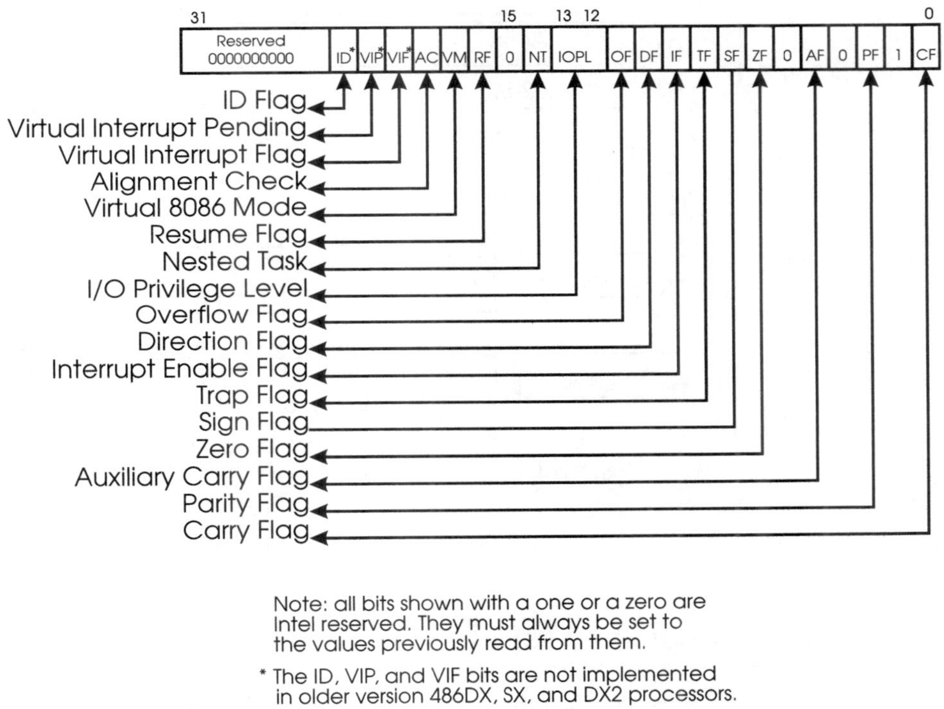

Figure 7-3. 486 EFlags Register Definition

The System-Level Registers

Figure 7-4 illustrates the 80486 system-level registers. These registers are the same as those implemented in the 80386 microprocessors. However, the 486 has redefined some bits in CR0 and CR3 and has added CR4. The following sections summarize the functions of each system-level register, details the changes implemented in CR0 and CR3, and defines the new CR4.

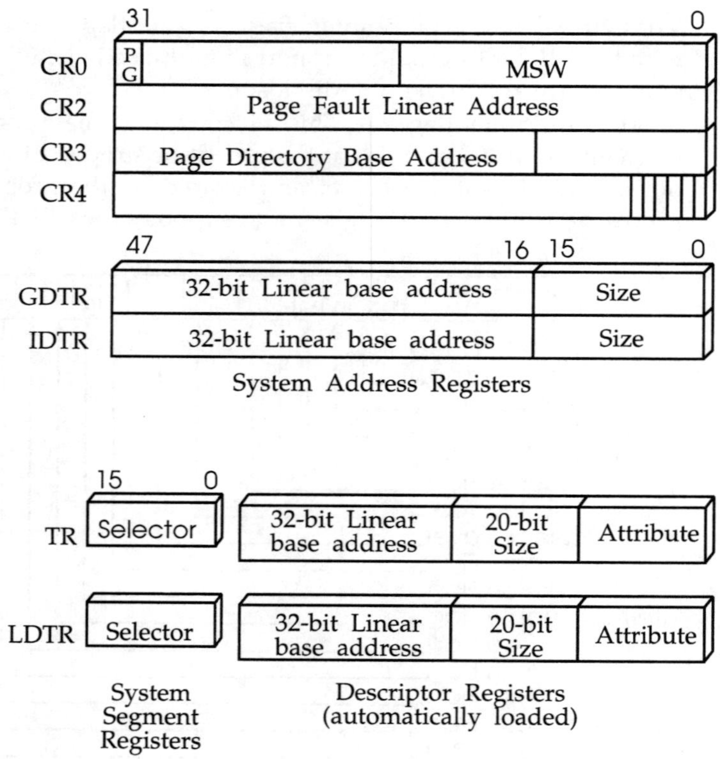

Figure 7-4. 80486 System Registers

Control Register 0 (CR0)

Five new, 80486-specific bits have been added to CR0 including:

- CD — cache disable
- NW — not write through
- AM — alignment mask
- WP — write protect
- NE — numeric exception

Figure 7-5 illustrates the format of CR0. Each new bit is described in the following sections.

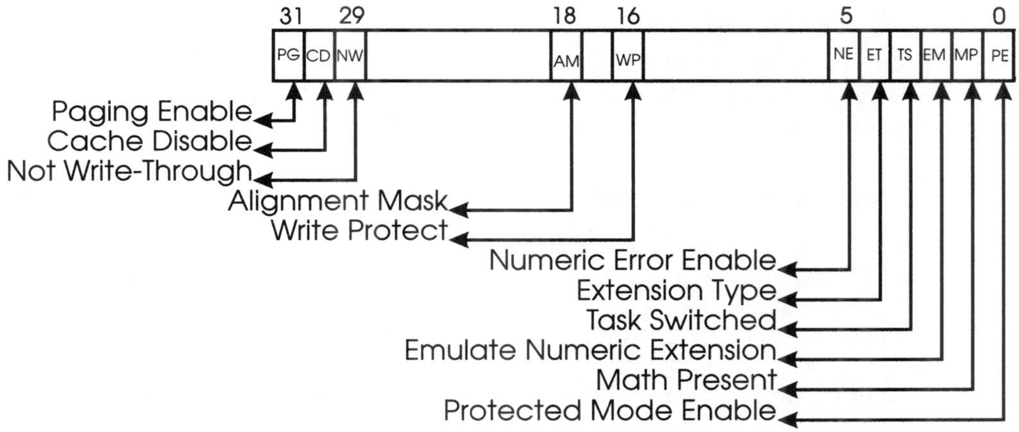

Figure 7-5. Bit definition for CR0

Cache Disable (CD) and Not Write-Through (NW)

The CD and NW bits are used to control the internal cache. Table 7-1 defines the cache modes selected by all settings of these two control bits.

Table 7-1. Cache Control Bits

CD	NW	Operating Mode
1	1	Cache fills disabled; write-through and invalidates disabled.
1	0	Cache fills disabled; write-through and invalidates enabled.
0	1	Invalid. If CR0 is loaded with this combination, a GP (General Protection) Fault with an error code of 0 is raised.
0	0	Cache fills enabled; write-through and invalidates enabled.

Alignment Mask (AM)

The alignment mask bit enables or disables alignment checking. If the AM bit is cleared to 0, the AC bit in the EFLAGS register is ignored and alignment checking isn't performed. If set to 1 in the AM bit allows the AC bit in EFLAGS to control alignment checking.

Write-Protect (WP)

This bit protects read-only memory pages from supervisor (operating system) write access. Setting WP to a 1 enables error reporting when a supervisor attempts to write the respective memory page.

Numeric Exception (NE)

This bit controls whether floating-point errors are reported using the DOS-compatible method (IRQ13) or by generating an exception 16 interrupt. Setting this bit to 1 causes the microprocessor to generate an internal exception 16 interrupt when the floating-point unit incurs an error.

If the programmer wishes the processor to use the PC-DOS-compatible error reporting technique for floating-point errors, this bit should be reset to 0. PC-DOS uses interrupt request level 13 to report this type of error.

In either case, a floating-point error causes the microprocessor's FERR# output to go active. This pin is the equivalent of the 287/387 ERROR output.

The 80486 also has an input pin called IGNNE#. If this pin is inactive (high), the 80486 microprocessor freezes immediately before executing the next floating-point instruction and an interrupt is generated. It will be an exception 16 interrupt if the NE bit is set to 1. If NE is reset to 0, an exception interrupt will not be generated. Instead, an external 8259 Programmable Interrupt Controller (PIC) will sense IRQ13 (from the microprocessor's FERR# output) and the interrupt will be handled as an external hardware interrupt.

If the microprocessor's IGNNE# input is set active and a floating-point error is encountered, the microprocessor ignores the error and continues to execute floating-point instructions.

Control Register 2 (CR2)

CR2 holds the 32-bit linear address that caused the last page fault detected. The error code pushed onto the page fault handler's stack when it's invoked provides additional status information regarding this fault.

Control Register 3 (CR3)

CR3 is the page directory base address register. The format of CR3 is illustrated in figure 7-6. It contains the following information:

- Page Directory Base Address — The upper 20 bits of CR3 contain the memory start address of the page directory. The processor assumes that the lower twelve bits of the address are zero. This allows the programmer to indicate the start address on any 4KB address boundary.
- PCD (Page Cache Disable) — This bit controls cacheability of the page directory.
- PWT (Page Write-Through) — This bit controls the write policy to be used by an external write-back cache when the processor updates the page directory.

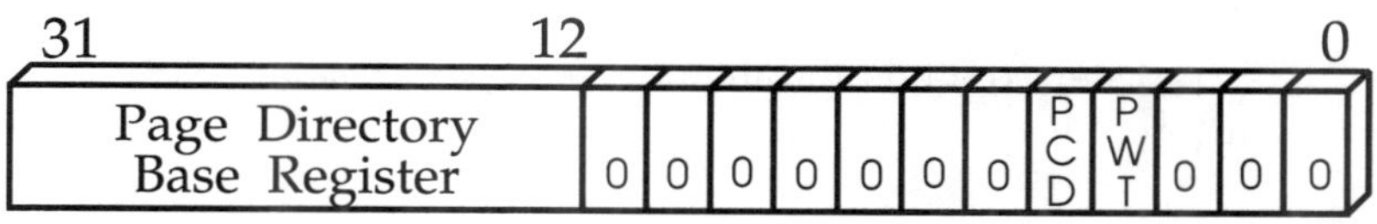

Figure 7-6. Format of CR3

Control Register 4 (CR4)

Control Register four has been added to enable and disable new processor extensions. The format of CR4 is illustrated in figure 7-7. The new bits include:

- PSE (Page Size Extensions) — This bit permits the processor to support 4MB pages in addition to 4KB pages.
- PVI (Protected mode Virtual Interrupts) — This bit enables support for the virtual interrupt flag (VIF) in protected mode. Details regarding the implementation of virtual interrupts is not disclosed by Intel.
- VME (Virtual 8086 Mode Extensions) — This bit enables the processor to support the virtual interrupt flag (VIF) when the processor is in virtual 8086 mode. Details regarding the implementation of virtual interrupts is not disclosed by Intel.

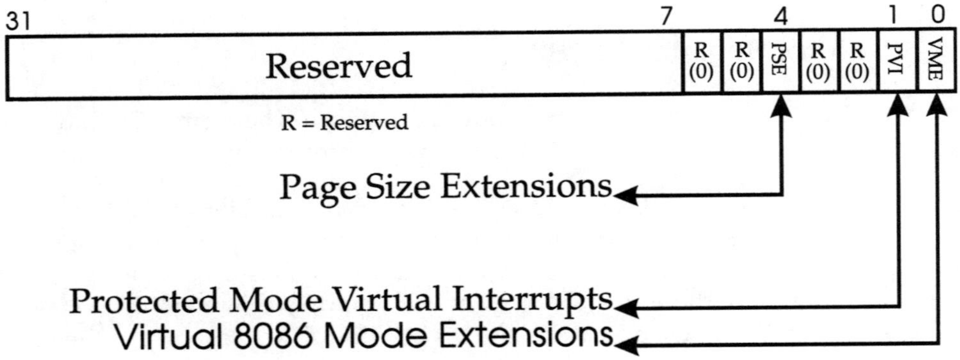

Figure 7-7. Format of CR4

Global Descriptor Table Register (GDTR)

This register contains the memory base address and length of the global descriptor table.

Interrupt Descriptor Table Register (IDTR)

This register contains the memory base address and length of the interrupt descriptor table.

Task State Segment Register (TR)

The 16-bit value in this register identifies a descriptor in the Global Descriptor Table (GDT) that describes the task state segment.

Local Descriptor Table Register (LDTR)

This register contains the memory base address and length of the local descriptor table.

Virtual Paging

Both the 80386 and the 80486 microprocessors incorporate logic to facilitate the implementation of virtual paging (also referred to as demand paging) in an operating system. Paging is enabled by turning on the PG bit in CR0 (bit 31). When enabled, the address produced by the segmentation unit, called the linear address, is used as an input to the paging unit. The linear address output by the segmentation unit is used by the paging unit to identify a page table, a page described within that table, and an offset, or location, within that page. (Refer to MindShare's *ISA System Architecture* book, published by Addison-Wesley, for a detailed discussion of virtual paging.)

The 80486 microprocessor implements additional bits (not present in the 80386) to indicate page cacheability for the internal and external caches and write-policy for external write-back caches. These new bits, PCD (page cache disable) and PWT (page write-through), are defined in CR3, the page directory entries, and the page table entries.

The 486 paging mechanism in new generation 486 processors also support the 4MB paging feature that was introduced in the Pentium processor. This permits the operating system to specify either 4KB or 4MB pages.

The page directory entry has the format illustrated in table 7-1. It should be noted that page directory and page table entries have the same format.

Table 7-1. Format of Page Directory or Page Table Entry

Bit(s)	ID	Definition
0	P	The **page present** bit. Will be set to a 1 if the main memory page containing the target Page Table is currently resident in main memory. Set to 0 if the page containing the target Page Table must be read from disk.
1	R/W	The **read/write** bit. When set to 1, it is permitted to both read and write the target page. Set to 0, the page can only be read.
2	U/S	The **user/supervisor** bit. A 1 in this bit indicates that the page is accessible by both the operating system and applications programs. Set to 0, it indicates that the page may only be accessed by the operating system.
3	PCD	0 = page is cacheable; 1 = page isn't cacheable.

Table 7-1, continued

Bit(s)	ID	Definition
4	PWT	0 = external cache controller should use write-back policy to handle memory writes; 1 = external cache controller should use write-through policy to handle memory writes.
5	A	The **accessed** bit. Set by hardware before a read or write access to the target page. The operating system can use the state of this bit to determine whether the page is being used (accessed). If it isn't, the operating system may choose to read a different page from disk into this 4KB page of main memory.
6	D	The **dirty** bit. This bit is undefined in a page directory entry. In a page table entry, the dirty bit is set before a write to the page described by the page table entry. When set, indicates that the operating system should insure that the page is written back to disk to maintain coherency between disk and main memory.
7:8	none	not used.
9:11	none	These three bits aren't used by the 80386/80486 microprocessor. They may be used by the system programmer in a programmer-specified fashion.
12:31	none	In a page directory entry, this field supplies the upper 20 bits of the page table start address. In a Page Table entry, this field supplies the upper 20 bits of the start address of the page in memory. The lower twelve bits of the start address are assumed to be zero.

The Floating-Point Registers

The operation of the 80486's on-chip floating-point unit (FPU) is identical with that of the 387.

Refer to figure 7-8. As illustrated, the on-chip floating-point unit contains:

- Eight data registers. Each of these registers contains an 80-bit representation of a floating-point number. The 80-bits are divided into three fields: Sign, Exponent and Significand.
- Tag word. The tag word is actually divided into eight 2-bit tag fields, each of which is associated with one of the data registers. The principle function of the tag bits are to optimize the FPU's performance and stack-

handling by making it possible to distinguish between empty and full register locations. It also allows exception handlers to check the contents of a register location without the need to perform complex decoding of the actual data.

- Control register. The FPU provides several processing options that are selected by loading a control word from memory into the control register.
- The low-order byte of the FPU control register configures the FPU error and exception masking. Bits 0:5 contain individual masks for each of the six exceptions that the FPU recognizes.
- The high-order byte of the control register configures the FPU operating mode, including precision and rounding.
- Status register. Reflects the overall state of the FPU.
- Instruction pointer register. Because the FPU operates in parallel with the execution unit, any errors reported by the FPU may be reported after the microprocessor's ALU has executed the FPU instruction that caused it. To allow identification of the failing instruction, the 80486 microprocessor contains two pointer registers that supply the address of the failing instruction and the address of its numeric memory operand (if appropriate).
- The instruction and data pointer registers are provided for user-written error handlers. Whenever the 80486 microprocessor decodes a new floating-point instruction, it saves the instruction (including any prefixes that may be present), the address of the operand (if present) and the opcode.
- Data pointer register. See explanation of the instruction pointer register above.

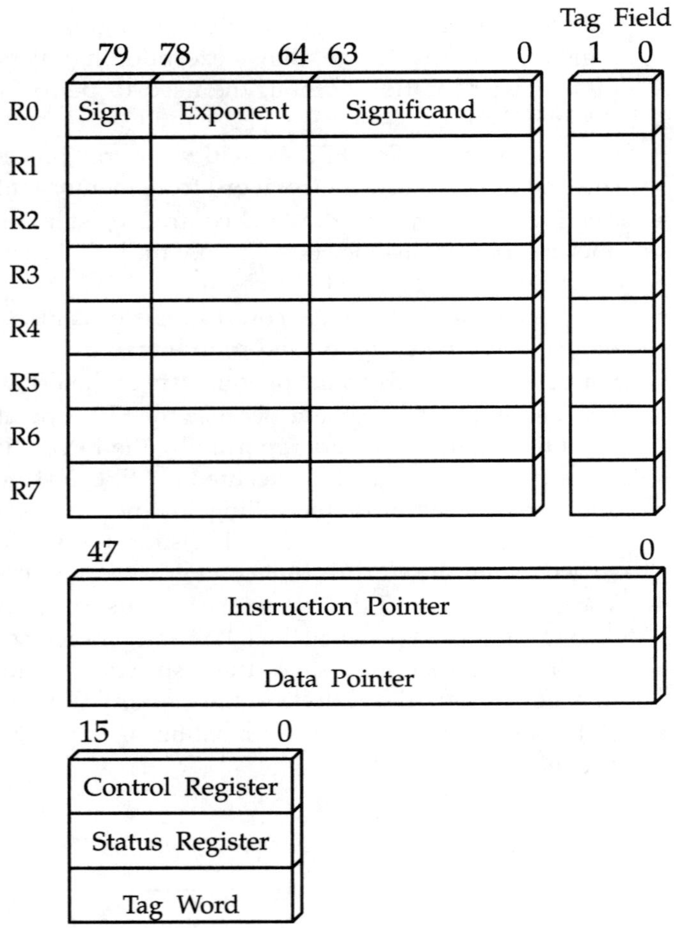

Figure 7-8. The 80486 Floating-Point Registers

The Debug and Test Registers

Refer to figure 7-9. The six programmer-accessible debug registers provide on-chip support for debugging and are present in both the 80386 and 80486. Debug registers DR3:DR0 specify the four linear breakpoint addresses. The breakpoint control register, DR7, is used to set the breakpoints, define them as data or code breakpoints, and whether to break on an attempted read or write. The breakpoint status register, DR6, reflects the current state of the breakpoints.

The 80486 also contains five test registers, TR7:TR3. TR6 and TR7 are used to control the testing of the Translation Lookaside Buffer (TLB) and are found in both the 80386 and 80486. TR3, TR4 and TR5 are used for testing the on-chip cache and are only found in the 80486 and Pentium processors.

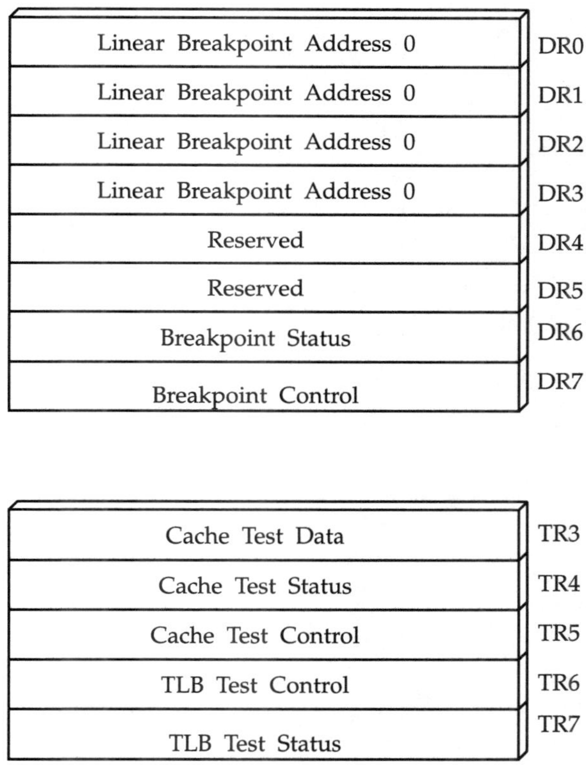

Figure 7-9. The 80486 Debug and Test Registers

Chapter 8

The Previous Chapter

This previous chapter discussed the changes to the x86 software environment that were introduced and implemented in the latest 486DX processors.

This Chapter

This chapter introduces the 486SX and 487SX processors and highlights the differences between the 486SX processors and the 486DX processors.

The Next Chapter

The next chapter introduces the 486DX2 and 486SX2 processors and highlights the differences between them and the 486DX and 486SX processors.

Introduction to the 80486SX and 80487SX Processors

The 80486SX microprocessor is essentially an 80486DX microprocessor without the Floating-Point Unit. A system based on an 80486SX microprocessor could be upgraded to an 80486DX microprocessor if the chips were pin-compatible, but they aren't. In order to upgrade an 80486SX-based system to incorporate the full capabilities of the 80486DX, a second chip, the 80487SX, must be installed in another socket. Essentially, the 80487SX is an 80486DX microprocessor with altered pinouts. This new socket has been dubbed the "performance" socket by Intel. Installing the 80487SX in the "performance" socket effectively disables the 80486SX forever. The 80487SX then becomes the system microprocessor, complete with floating-point capability.

On the surface, Intel's strategy may not seem to make sense, but consider these points:

- If an 80486SX system could be upgraded to an 80486DX by simply replacing the microprocessor chip, the 80486SX microprocessors that were removed during the upgrade process could then be sold on the gray market.
- If end-users were to attempt the upgrade on their own, they could damage the microprocessor's pins and/or the socket, thus voiding their warranty.

Some system vendors however, use a single-socket approach, where a special socket accepts either the 486DX or the 486SX microprocessor. The "performance" or upgrade sockets allow customers to upgrade to the next generation processors without replacing the system board. Systems that do not incorporate the upgrade sockets cannot be upgraded.

Because the 80486SX doesn't incorporate the floating-point unit, systems based on this product will not perform as well as those based on the 80486DX when executing floating-point intensive applications. With the addition of an 80487SX "coprocessor", however, the performance of the systems would be identical (given an identical clock rate).

The 486SX Signal Interface

The only signal change between the 486DX and 486SX processors are those dedicated for floating-point functionality. A 486SX processor, having no floating-point unit, does not implement the FERR# and IGNNE# signals that are present on the 486DX.

Register Differences

The effect of some bits within CR0 differ between the 486DX and SX processors. These bits include:

- NE (Numeric Exception)
- TS (Task Switch)
- EM (Emulate Coprocessor)
- MP (Monitor Coprocessor)

These bit determine how the processor responds when floating-point instructions and the WAIT instruction are executed. The 486SX behaves similar to the earlier processors (i.e. the 80386) when no external numeric co-processor was installed. Both systems generate exceptions when floating-point instructions are encountered and expect software to emulate the instruction. (See MindShare's *ISA System Architecture* book, published by Addison-Wesley, for a description of floating-point emulation).

Chapter 9

The Previous Chapter

The previous chapter introduced the 486 SX processor and detailed the differences between it and the 486DX.

This Chapter

This chapter introduces the 486DX2 and 486SX2 processors and highlights the differences between them and the 486DX and SX processors.

The Next Chapter

This chapter discusses the features associated with the Enhanced Write Back 486DX2 and the differences between it and the standard 486DX2 processors. The chapter focuses on new signals, the MESI model, special cycles, and cache line fill and snoop transactions.

The Clock Doubler Processors

Designing system boards around microprocessors running at extremely high clock rates is a challenging and time-consuming task. The signal traces on the system board that carry the very high frequency clock signals required by these processors produce a large amount of EMI (electro-magnetic interference), interfering with other system components and radiating into the surrounding area. System layout becomes extremely critical and sophisticated shielding techniques must be employed to reduce the EMI's affects on the system and the surrounding environment.

In order to address this problem, Intel added the DX2 and SX2 processors to the 80486 family of processors. Internally, these processors incorporate an internal Phase-Lock Loop (PLL) designed to double the frequency of the clock signal supplied to the microprocessor by the off-chip crystal oscillator. All operations performed within the microprocessor are therefore executed at double the speed achievable by an 80486 that does not incorporate the clock-doubler capability. The 80486 processor incorporates the floating-point unit and an on-chip 8KB four-way set associative cache subsystem. All floating-point execution, operations involving only the processor's internal registers, and operations accessing memory locations already cached in the internal cache benefit from the clock-doubler or overdrive feature.

When the processor must access an external device, however, the resultant bus cycle takes place at the rated speed of the processor's clock input, not at the doubled rate. For example, the first version of the clock-doubler 80486 was the 80486-25DX2. Supplied with a 25MHz input clock, this chip operates at the internal rate of 50MHz and runs bus cycles at the rate of 25MHz. This allows the system board designer to use parts rated at the 25MHz speed, while still achieving 50MHz operation within the processor's core.

Intel supplies two basic versions of clock doubler processors:

- One version adheres to the "performance" socket pinout and can be used to upgrade systems based on the 80486SX processor.
- The other version implements an 80486DX upgrade socket. This socket can be implemented as a separate socket on the system board, or as a single socket that allows direct replacement of the 80486DX processor.

Although the DX2 will act as a direct replacement of the current processor, many systems ship with a DX2 processor. Upgrades for these systems are still possible with a DX4 processor.

Note that a few problems that must be considered with upgrade solutions:

- The increased internal speed of the clock-doubler processor produces substantially more heat than the processor it replaces. This means a heat-sink and possibly additional cooling may be required. In addition, the clock-doubler version uses substantially more power. As an example, the original 80486DX2 66MHz processor uses approximately 40% more power than a 33MHz 486DX.
- The ROM BIOS may contain subroutines that depend on instruction execution timing loops to perform some functions. Substitution of the clock-doubler chip could therefore result in erratic operation of the ROM BIOS, requiring changes in the ROM BIOS.

Chapter 10

The Previous Chapter

The previous chapter introduced the clock doubler processors known as the 486DX2 and 486SX2. The differences between these processors and the 486DX and 486SX are highlighted.

This Chapter

This chapter discusses the features associated with the Enhanced Write Back 486DX2 and the differences between it and the standard 486DX2 processors. The chapter focuses on new signals, the MESI model, special cycles, and cache line fill and snoop transactions.

The Next Chapter

The next chapter overviews the 486DX4 processor and discusses the differences between the it and the 486DX2 processors.

Introduction to the Write Back Enhanced 486DX2

The Write-back Enhanced 486DX2 implements an 8KB unified internal cache organized as 4-way set associative with 16 byte cache lines, which is exactly the same as the 486DX, 486SX, 486SX2 and other 486DX2 processors. The only difference is the write-back policy supported by the Write Back Enhanced 486DX2. The write policy is selectable at reset, allowing the Enhanced Write 486DX2 to be configured for the write-through policy (like the other 486 processors) or the write-back policy (similar to the Pentium processors).

Like the Pentium processor the MESI cache states are employed to define the write policy to be used on a line-by-line basis. However, unlike the Pentium processor, this processor is not intended to be used in multiprocessor implementations. As a result, the actual MESI protocol implemented by the

Enhance Write Back 486 does not include transitions to the "S" state during snoop operations.

To support the write-back capability new interface pins have also been defined. The following sections detail the operation of the Enhanced Write Back 486DX2 processor, focusing on the differences between it and other 486 processors.

Advantage of the Write-Back Policy

The write-back policy reduces the number of 486 write bus transfers to main memory when compared with the write-through policy. Overall system performance can be improved in systems that employ multiple bus masters on the expansion bus (e.g. PCI, VESA VL, and EISA). Consider the requirements and related system performance of each write-policy as discussed below.

The Write-Through Policy

When a write-through policy is used, any write transfer that hits the internal cache updates the internal cache line, and the 486 processor must also generate a memory write bus cycle to write the data on through to main memory. This ensures that other bus masters residing on the expansion bus (e.g.) can access memory without causing potential cache coherency problems. While the write-through policy simplifies the job of maintaining cache coherency, the system buses are occupied with a write bus cycle every time the processor performs a memory write transfer, whether the write hits the internal cache or not. This may cause other bus masters in the system to stall a large percentage of the time, waiting for the processor to relinquish control of the system bus. As a result, the system's performance is adversely affected by the large number of write transfers occurring to main memory.

Most of these write transfers performed by the 486 processor are not necessary, since they are writes to memory locations that other bus masters will never access. This means that the write-through policy while effective in eliminating potential cache consistency problems, is not efficient from a bus utilization perspective.

The Write-Back Policy

In contrast, the write-back policy permits the processor to update a cache line that hits the internal cache without having to write the data on through to main memory. This reduces the number of write bus cycles that the processor performs, leaving the buses free for other bus masters to use. Since the processor updates the copy of a memory location within cache, but not main memory, the write-back policy leaves main memory with stale data. To preserve cache coherency, the processor must be able to detect when another bus master accesses (read or write) a memory location that contains stale data. The processor must notify the system that a bus master is accessing a location containing stale data (in response the system must back the bus master off), and write the contents of the modified cache line to memory. Once the cache line has been written back to memory, the system releases the back-off, allowing the bus master to complete the transfer to memory.

The mechanism used to maintain cache coherency when the write-back policy is used may seem very complex and time consuming, and perhaps not worth the effort. Consider, however that an extremely large percentage of the memory writes that the processor performs are to locations that other bus masters never access. Furthermore, the number of locations shared between the processor and other bus masters is quite small as is the percentage of overall accesses to these shared locations.

Signal Interface

The following sections describe the new signals implemented by the Write Back Enhanced 486DX2 processor, along with other signals whose functions have been modified.

New Signals

The new signals supporting the write-back operation of the internal cache are:

- CACHE#
- HITM#
- INV
- WB/WT#

These signals function is the same manner as they do on the Pentium Over-Drive processor that is designed as a 486 system upgrades. Each signal is described in table 10-1.

Table 10-1. Signals Supporting Write-Back Policy

Signal	I/O	Description
CACHE#	O	Asserted by the microprocessor at the beginning of the bus cycle to indicate that it wishes to perform a burst transfer. These transfers include cache line fills and write-back cycles both of which are 16-byte transfers.
HITM#	O	**Hit modified** is asserted by the microprocessor to indicate that a snoop to its internal cache hit a line stored in the "M" state. If a snoop hits a cache line stored in any other state HITM# remains deasserted.
INV	I	**Invalidate** is asserted by external logic during snoop operation to specify whether the processor should invalidate or retain the copy of a line that was hit during a snoop. INV=1 — External logic asserts INV when it detects another bus master writing to main memory, forcing the processor to invalidate it copy of the cache line. This is termed an invalidation cycle. INV=0 — External logic deasserts INV when it detects another bus master reading from main memory, permitting the processor to keep a copy of the cache line. This is termed an inquire cycle.
WB/WT#	I	The **write-back or write-through** pin is sampled by the processor when RESET is asserted to specify whether the processor will operate in a write-through mode (like all other 486 processors) or will operate in enhanced bus mode, thereby using a write-back cache policy. When the write-back policy is selected, the WB/WT# pin is sampled during cache line fills to determine the write policy (MESI state) to be used with the line currently being read from memory. WB/WT# is sampled in the same clock that the first RDY# or BRDY# of a cache line fill is sampled.

Existing Signals with Modified Functionality

Several signals implemented on the Write Back Enhanced 486DX2 are not new to 486 processors, but in some way their function or definition has changed. These signals include:

- Flush# — when FLUSH# is asserted the processor writes back all modified lines in the internal cache before invalidating the entries. This is followed by two special bus cycles. See the section entitled, "Special Cycles" later in this chapter for details.
- PLOCK# — when the processor is in enhanced bus mode PLOCK# remains inactive.
- SRESET — asserting SRESET has the same effect as it does with other 486 processors, plus it does not disable the cache, write-back modified lines, or invalidate the cache's contents.

The MESI Model

The MESI model was created primarily to support multiprocessing systems, but is used by the Enhanced Write Back 486DX2 processor in single-processor systems. The MESI model defines four states that a given cache line can be stored in within the Write Back Enhanced 486DX2's internal cache. Refer to table 10-2. The MESI bit determines the action to be taken by the processor when it reads from or writes to a cache line.

Table 10-2. The MESI State Definitions

State	Write Policy	Definition
Modified	WB	The line in cache has been updated (contains modified data) due to a write hit in the cache. The processor when writing to this line will update the line but not generate a write bus cycle. Snoop hits to this line causes the processor to generate a write-back cycle to write the contents of the cache line back to memory.

Table 10-2, continued

State	Write Policy	Definition
Exclusive	WB	The contents of the cache line are the same as external memory. Also indicates that the processor upon writing to this line will update the line but not generate a write bus cycle. Snoops that hit a cache line in the E state need not be written back since they contain no modified data.
Shared	WT	The contents of the cache line are the same as external memory and the write-through policy is specified. The processor when writing to this line will update the line and generate a write to update main memory.
Invalid	WT	The initial state after reset, indicating that the line does not contain a valid copy of information contained in memory. Both reads or writes generate bus cycles.

Every line in cache is assigned one of the MESI state indicators to identify the status of the information stored in cache. Table 10-3 defines specifies the action taken by the processor along with the MESI bit transition that occurs during processor reads, writes, and snoops.

Table 10-3. MESI States and Resulting Action by Processor During Reads, Writes, and Snoops that Access a Cache Line

State	Action Taken by Processor When it Accesses Line
Modified	**Read** — processor accesses target location(s) from cache line and no bus cycle is generated. No MESI state change. **Write** — processor updates the line but does not generate a write bus cycle. No MESI state change. **Snoop resulting from external read** — snoop hits cause the processor to generate a write-back cycle to write the contents of the cache line back to memory. Cache line transitions back to the "E" state. **Snoop resulting from external write** — snoop hits cause the processor to generate a write-back cycle to write the contents of the cache line back to memory. The cache line transitions to the "I" state.

Table 10-3, continued

State	Action Taken by Processor When it Accesses Line
Exclusive	**Read** — processor accesses target location from cache line and no bus cycle is generated. No MESI state change. **Write** — processor updates the line and no bus cycle is generated. MESI state transitions to "M" **Snoop resulting from external read** — snoop hits result in no action by the processor. No MESI state change. **Snoop resulting from external write** — snoop hits cause the processor to transition the MESI state to "I" and no bus cycle is generated.
Shared	**Read** — processor accesses target location from cache line and no bus cycle is generated. No MESI state change. **Write** — processor updates the line and no bus cycle is generated. MESI state transitions to the "M" state. **Snoop resulting from external read** — snoop hits result in no action by the processor. No MESI state change. **Snoop resulting from external write** — snoop hits cause the processor to transition the MESI state to "I" and no bus cycle is generated.
Invalid	**Read** — Bus cycle is generated to access target location from memory. If location is cacheable processor performs a cache line fill and the state of the new cache line is determined by the state of WB/WT#. If WB/WT#=1, then line is stored in the "E" state. If WB/WT#=0, then line is stored in the "S" state. **Write** — Bus cycle is generated. No MESI state change. **Snoop resulting from external read** — snoop hits result in miss with no action by the processor. No MESI state change. **Snoop resulting from external write** — snoop hits result in miss with no action by the processor. No MESI state change.

Write Back Enhanced 486DX2 System without an L2 Cache

Figure 10-1 illustrates an example system design that does not incorporate a level 2 (L2) cache subsystem. As discussed previously, write-back designs improve overall system performance by updating memory only when necessary, thereby keeping the system bus free for use by other processors and bus masters. Main memory is updated (written to) only when:

- Another bus master initiates a read access to a memory line that contains stale data.
- Another bus master initiates a write access to a memory line that contains stale data.
- A cache line that contains modified information is about to be overwritten in order to store a line newly acquired from memory.

Cache lines are marked as modified (M) in the cache directory when they are updated by the processor. When another master is reading from or writing to memory, the cache subsystem must monitor, or snoop, the system bus to check for memory accesses to lines marked as modified in the cache.

Write-back cache designs are more complicated to implement than write-through designs because they must make decisions on when to write modified lines back to memory to ensure cache consistency. The following sections define several scenarios that describe actions taken by the processor when configured for write-back enhanced bus operation.

Cache Line Fill

Line fills can occur when the cache is enabled (CD and NW bits in CR0 are zero), when the software has indicated cacheability (relevant PCD bits are asserted), and when external logic has agreed that the target locations can be cached (KEN# is asserted).

Figure 10-2 illustrates a sample cache line fill bus cycle with the processor in the write back enhanced mode. Cache line fills performed by the Write Back Enhanced 486DX2 are similar to those performed by other 486 processors. A cache line fill request is passed to the processor's bus unit after a memory read instruction has been submitted to the internal cache, resulting in a read miss.

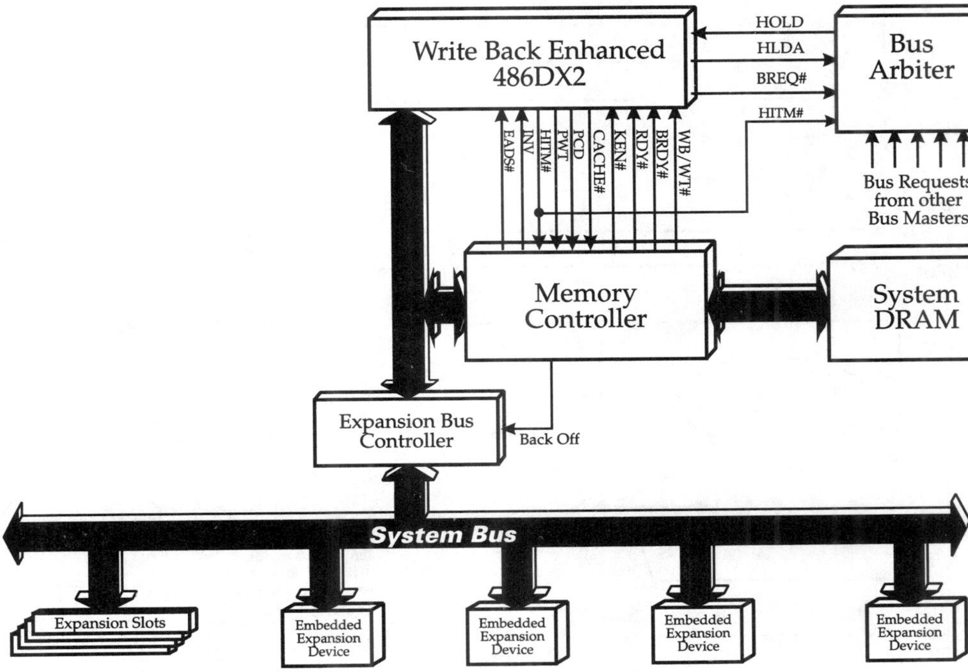

Figure 10-1. Example of System with Write Back Enhanced 486DX2 (no L2 Cache)

Note that the line fill operation illustrated in figure 10-2 appears exactly as it would with any other 486 processor with the following differences.

1. The write back enhanced processor asserts the CACHE# signal when beginning a cache line fill operation. Note the CACHE# remains asserted until the first ready (RDY# or BRDY#) is returned asserted.

2. The processor samples WB/WT# in the same clock as the first ready is returned. The state of WB/WT# specifies which MESI state the processor should store the line in. In figure 10-2, the processor detects that the line should be stored in the E (exclusive) state.

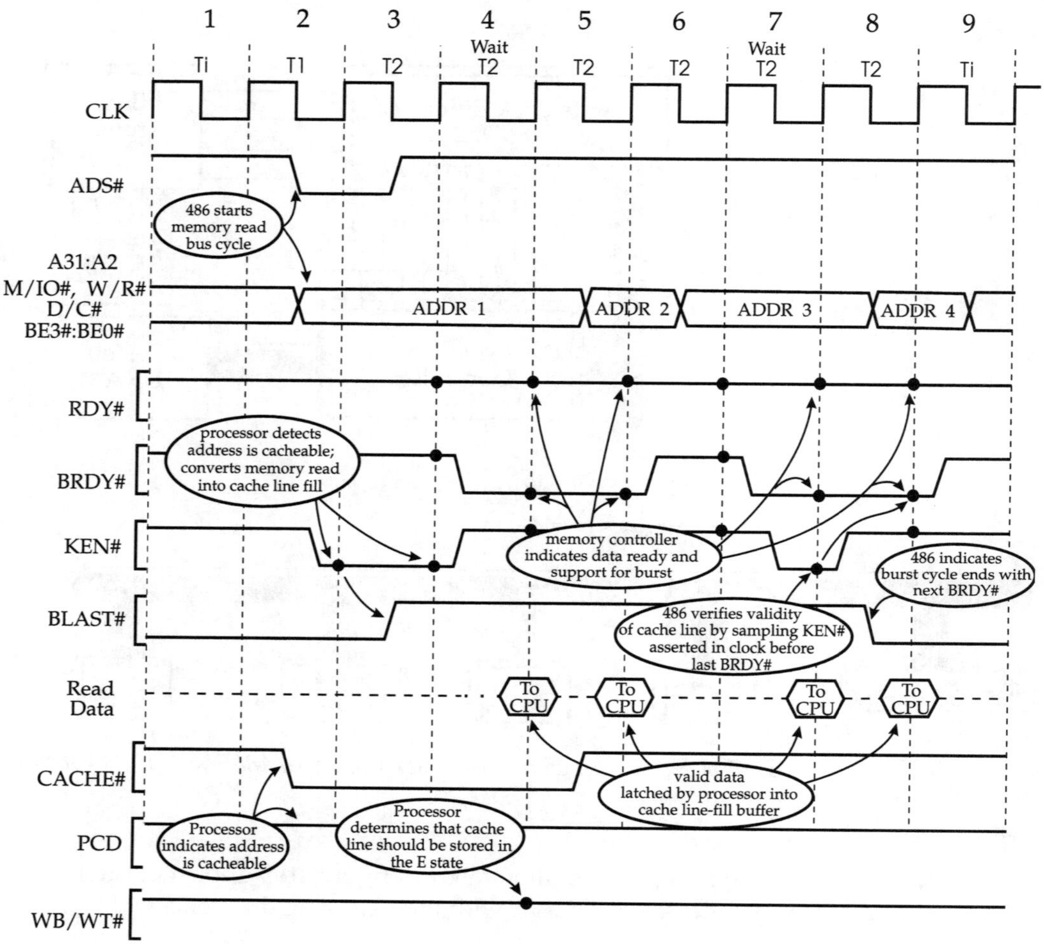

Figure 10-2. Example Cache Line Fill — Write-Back Mode Enabled

Bus Master Read — Processor Snoop

Other 486 processor do not perform snoop cycles resulting from other bus master reading from main memory. Snooping reads is not necessary since the write-through policy guarantees that external memory always has the latest information. The write-back policy however, requires that reads be snooped since a memory location being read by another bus master might contain stale data. Stale data is created in memory when the processor executes a write instruction that hits an internal cache line that is stored in the E state. The processor updates the cache line and changes the MESI state to "M," but does not write the data on to memory.

Snoop cycles resulting from bus master reads are termed inquire cycles since the snoop is performed to determine if the target cache line contains modified data. If not, the read operation can complete and the data stored in the processors cache will still contain valid data. Figure 10-3 illustrates a snoop resulting from a bus master read from memory. In this example the bus master has obtained control of the system bus via the bus arbiter, which has asserted the processor's HOLD line. Since HOLD is asserted, the processor's AHOLD signal is not needed (its address bus is already floated and ready to accept a snoop address). The following steps describe the sample inquire cycle.

1. The memory controller detects the memory read and asserts EADS# to command the processor to snoop the bus master address. The INV signal is deasserted, indicating that the internal cache should retain the cache line in the event of a cache hit.

2. The processor uses the address on the bus (A31:A4) to check its cache directory to determine if it has a copy of the target memory location. The cache detects a hit to a modified line and transitions the line to the E state.

3. Processor asserts HITM# to inform the memory controller that it has a copy of the target cache line containing modified data. Two clock cycles after asserting EADS# the memory controller samples HITM#.

4. The bus arbiter detects that the processor has experienced a snoop hit to a modified cache line and must perform a cache write-back cycle. In response the arbiter deasserts HOLD, giving control of the bus back to the processor.

5. The memory controller backs the bus master off (usually via the expansion bus controller) to prevent it from reading stale data from memory.

6. The processor starts a write-back cycle by asserting ADS#, CACHE#, PCD, and PWT. The write-back cycle transfers the contents of the modified cache line to main memory, thereby eliminating the stale data. HITM# remains asserted until the last RDY# or BRDY# of the write-back cycle completes. The processor does not sample KEN# or WB/WT# during write-back transfers.

7. BRDY# is sampled asserted in the four consecutive clock starting with clock 8. When the last BRDY# is sampled asserted at the end of clock 11, the processor deasserts HITM#.

8. The bus arbiter detects that the write-back has completed and re-asserts HOLD to the processor. The memory controller also seeing HITM# deasserted removes the backoff from the bus master, allowing it to continue its memory read.

9. The bus master completes its read and obtains valid data from memory.

Bus Master Write — Processor Snoop

During a bus master write operation, the processor must also snoop the address. The actions taken by the memory controller and the processor are the same as the previous example except that the snoop is an invalidation cycle rather than an inquire cycle. Once the modified line has been written back to memory and the bus master has completed its write operation, the processor's cache line will contain stale data.

When the processor snoops a bus master writes to memory, the invalidation cycle is nearly identical to the inquire cycle illustrated in figure 10-3. The difference between the inquire and invalidation cycles are:

- INV is asserted, informing the processor that it should invalidate its copy of the cache line in the event of a snoop hit.
- The MESI state transitions from M to I since the processor samples INV asserted.

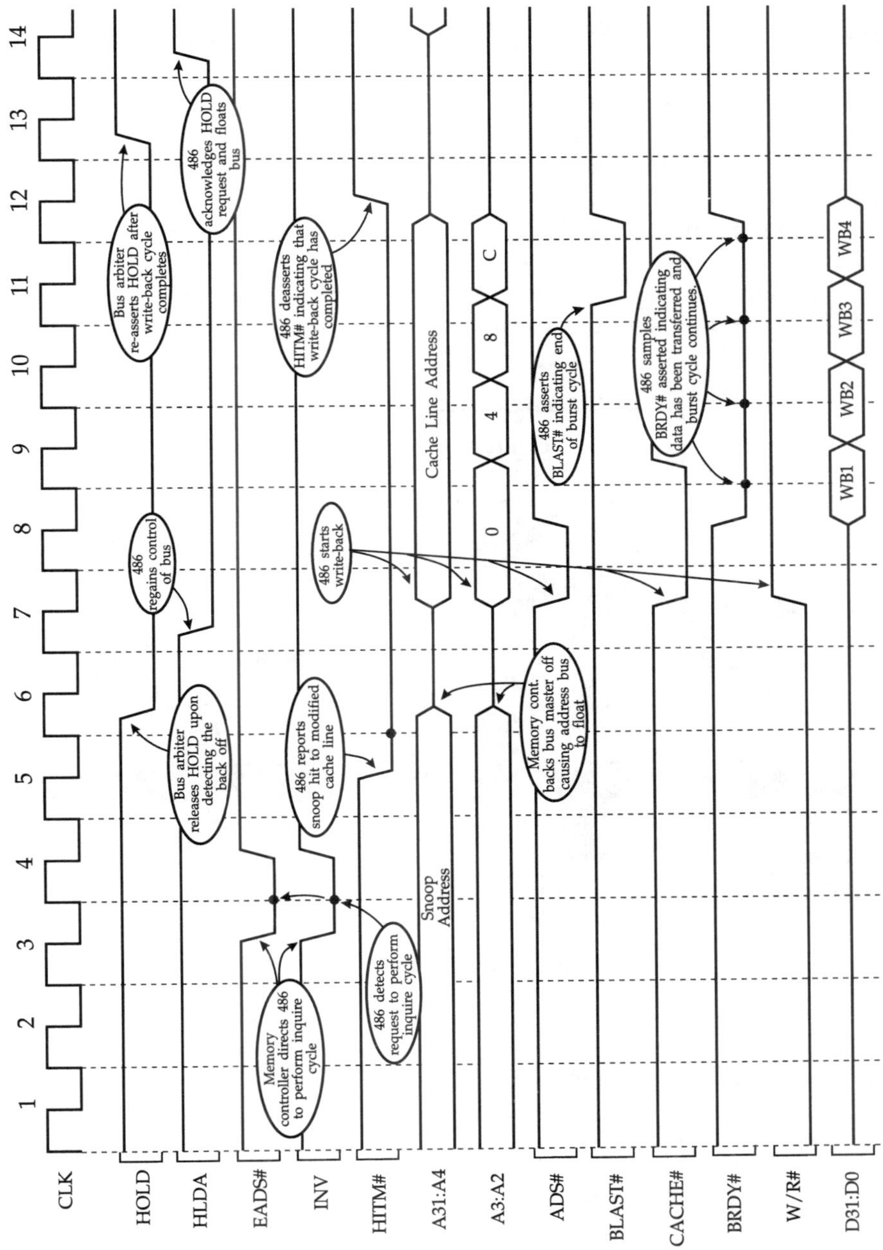

Figure 10-3. External Snoop Performed by Enhanced Write Back 486DX2 Processor

Write Back Enhanced 486DX2 System with an L2 Cache

The Write Back Enhanced 486DX2 may also be implemented in a system that contains an L2 cache subsystem. The L2 cache may be either a look-aside or look-through design. When a look-aside cache is implemented the processor behaves exactly as described in the previous example (no L2 cache was implemented). In both cases, the processor must relinquish control of the buses in order for another bus master to access memory. As a result, the AHOLD signal need not be implemented. Look-through cache designs however, allow concurrent bus operations, permitting the processor and other bus master transfers to overlap. The look-through cache configuration is illustrated in figure 10-4.

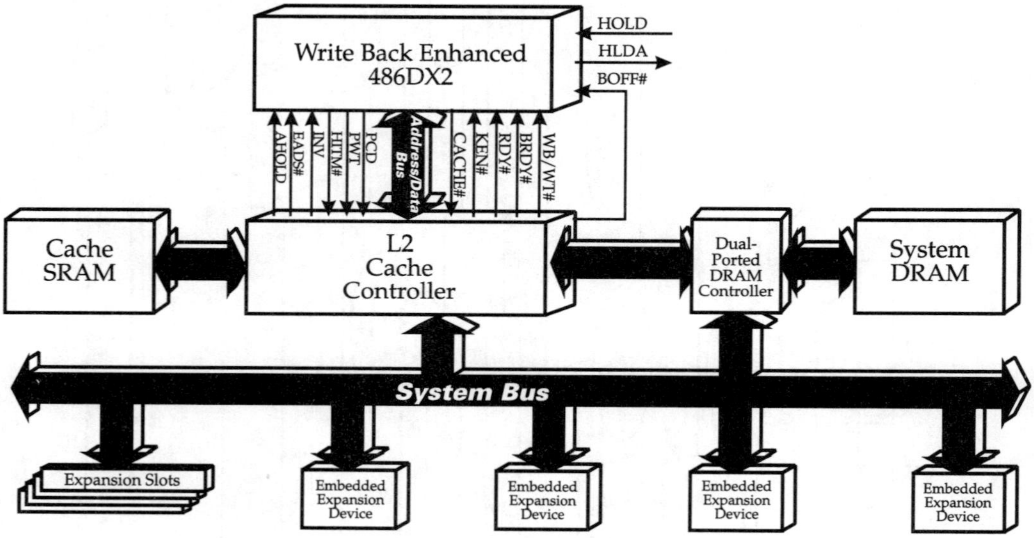

Figure 10-4. Write Back Enhanced 486 with Look-Through L2 Cache

A look-through L2 cache could be implemented with either a write-through or write-back policy. The following discussion summarizes the actions that would be taken by systems implementing each write policy when the processor implements a write-back policy.

The L2 Cache with a Write-Through Policy

An L2 cache controller implementing write-through policy in other 486 processor systems must snoop only bus master memory write transactions. Processor writes do not cause cache coherency problems because the 486 also implements a write-through policy. A memory write that hits the L1 cache updates the target line and transfers the processor's write transaction on to the L2 cache, which updates its cache line and transfers the write on to main memory. A bus master that reads from main memory will always obtain valid information due to the write-through policies of the L1 and L2 cache.

When a Write Back Enhanced 486 processor is configured to use a write-back policy, it updates its internal cache on a write instruction, but does not generate a write to update the L2 cache or main memory, leaving them both with stale data.

When a bus master reads from or writes to memory the L2 cache must snoop the address to detect if it has a copy of the target location. If the snoop hits the L2 cache, it recognizes that its cache and main memory may contain stale data. To prevent potential cache incoherency the L2 cache must take the following steps:

1. The L2 cache must back the bus master off and send an inquire cycle to the processor to determine if it has a modified copy of the target cache line.
2. The L2 cache monitors the processor's HITM# signal to detect the result of the snoop. If HITM# is deasserted, the L2 cache knows that the data contained in its cache and main memory is valid. If HITM# is asserted, the L2 cache awaits a write-back cycle from the processor so it can update its copy of the cache line and pass the cache line on to main memory.
3. Once the write-back to memory completes, back-off is removed from the bus master allowing it to complete its transfer.

The L2 Cache with a Write-Back Policy

The same set of considerations apply to an L2 write-back cache as apply to the L2 write-through cache described above. Additionally, the L2 write-back cache may also contain modified data. This occurs when the L1 cache replaces a cache line that the L2 cache retains. When the processor writes to a location within this line, the L1 cache will detect a miss and generate a memory write bus cycle. This write will hit the L2 cache which will update the cache line, transition the MESI bit to "M," but not write it through to main memory. The L2 write-back cache must be prepared to perform a write-back to main memory when a snoop hits a line in the "M" state. Like the write-through L2 cache, the write-back cache must snoop all bus master read and write transactions, and, if it detects a snoop hit, it passes the address to the L1 cache for snooping.

Note that the L2 write-back cache could be designed so that any snoop hit to a modified line be immediately written-back to memory. This is possible since the L2 cache controller can specify the write policy to be used by the 486's L1 cache during a cache line fill. If the cache line fill being performed is from an L2 cache line that is stored in the modified state, the L2 cache can pull the WB/WT# signal low during the first BRDY# returned by the L2 cache. This causes the 486 to store the cache line in the "S" state, forcing it to implement a write-through policy when writing to the cache line. In this way, the L2 cache guarantees that it will always have the latest information stored in its cache (because the processor must always write data through to the L2 cache). This permits the L2 cache to filter snoop read transfers (not run inquire cycles to the L1 cache) that hit a modified line in the L2 cache.

Snoop Cycle During Cache Line Fill

Figure 10-5 illustrates the Write Back Enhanced 486 processor performing a cache line fill when an external snoop occurs. In this example, another bus master in the system is writing to a memory location that the L2 cache controller has a copy of. The L2 cache must perform an invalidation cycle to direct the 486 to invalidate its copy of the cache line (if present). The L2 cache must also monitor the result of the snoop in case the 486 has modified its copy of the cache line. The following steps are taken by the system to ensure cache coherency is maintained.

1. The 486 processor starts a cache line fill sequence by asserting ADS#, CACHE#, and W/R# to the low state. At the same time, the L2 cache having detected a snoop hit resulting from a bus master write to memory and having backed the bus master off, asserts AHOLD to force the processor to float its address bus and prepare to receive a snoop address.
2. The L2 cache detects the 486 bus cycle, latches the address, and performs a lookup in its cache director to see if it has a copy of the cache line.
3. During clock 2 the processor floats its address bus in response to AHOLD. The L2 cache detects a read hit, returns the requested four bytes to the processor, asserts BRDY# and drives WB/WT# high.
4. The processor samples BRDY# and WB/WT# at the end of clock 2. Since WB/WT# is sampled high the processor knows to store the cache line in the "E" state when the cache line fill completes. BRDY# is sampled by the processor at the end of each clock cycle until the cache line fill completes at the end of clock 5.
5. During clock 3, the L2 cache asserts EADS# to command the processor to snoop the bus master address. The INV signal is also asserted, indicating that the internal cache should invalidate the cache line in the event of a cache hit.
6. The processor samples INV asserted at the end of clock 3 and uses the address on the bus (A31:A4) to check its cache directory to determine if it has a copy of the target memory location. The cache detects a hit to a modified line and transitions the line to the "I" state.
7. Processor asserts HITM# to inform the L2 cache that it has a copy of the target cache line containing modified data. Two clock cycles after asserting EADS# the L2 cache samples HITM# and recognizes that the processor will perform a cache write-back cycle.
8. The processor starts a write-back cycle in clock 7 by asserting ADS#, CACHE#, PCD, and PWT and drives W/R# to the high state. Note that the processor does not sample KEN# or WB/WT# during write-back transfers.
9. The L2 cache asserts BRDY# indicating that is has received the first 4 bytes of the write-back cycle and begins to transfer the write-back data on to slow DRAM memory.
10. The L2 cache asserts BRDY# in four consecutive clock cycles and latches the remaining bytes and the processor ends write-back cycle.
11. The processor deasserts HITM# at the end of the write-back cycle. The L2 cache however continues to perform the write-back cycle to main memory. When the L2 cache completes the write-back cycle to main memory, it removes the backoff from the bus master, allowing it to continue its memory write transfer.

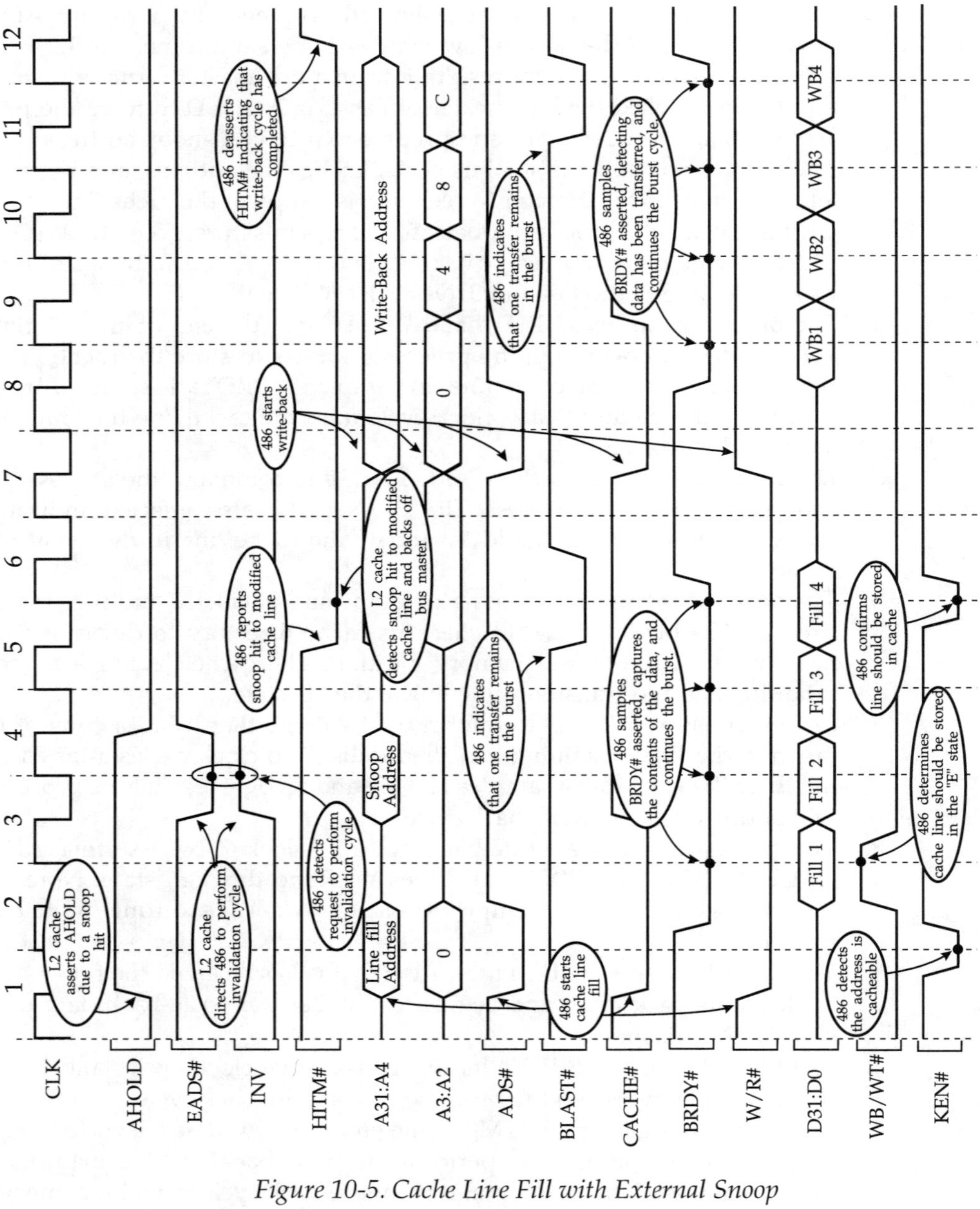

Figure 10-5. Cache Line Fill with External Snoop

Special Cycles

The Enhanced Write Back 486DX2 processor supports seven types of special cycles. Table 10-4 lists the types of special cycle supported. When the bus cycle definition lines indicate that a special cycle is being performed, the system must decode byte enable lines BE3#:BE0# and A2 as shown in table 10-4 to determine the type of special cycle being run.

The first and second flush acknowledge cycles are only used when the processor is in enhanced write mode. These special cycles are run when the FLUSH# pin is asserted. The processor writes-back all modified lines and then invalidates all entries within the cache. When the write-back and invalidate operation completes the processor performs the first flush acknowledge cycle followed by the second flush acknowledge cycle.

Note that the WBINVD instructions also causes the processor to first write-back all modified lines and invalidate the entire cache. However, the WBINVD instruction results in a write-back special cycle followed by a flush special cycle.

Table 10-4. Special Cycle Decoding

Special Cycle Type	BE3#	BE2#	BE1#	BE0#	A2
Shutdown	1	1	1	0	0
Flush	1	1	0	1	0
Second Flush Acknowledge*	1	1	0	1	1
Halt	1	0	1	1	0
Stop Grant Acknowledge	1	0	1	1	1
First Flush Acknowledge*	0	1	1	1	1
Write-back	0	1	1	1	0

* Defined only for the Enhanced Write Back 486DX2 processor.

Clock Control

The Enhanced Write Back 486DX2 includes the stop clock and auto HALT power down capability. Figure 10-6 illustrates the stop clock state machine transitions that occur when the processor is operating in the enhanced bus mode.

Changes to the clock state machine include:

- an additional state is added called the Auto HALT Power Down Flush State.
- redefinition of the Stop Clock Snoop state.

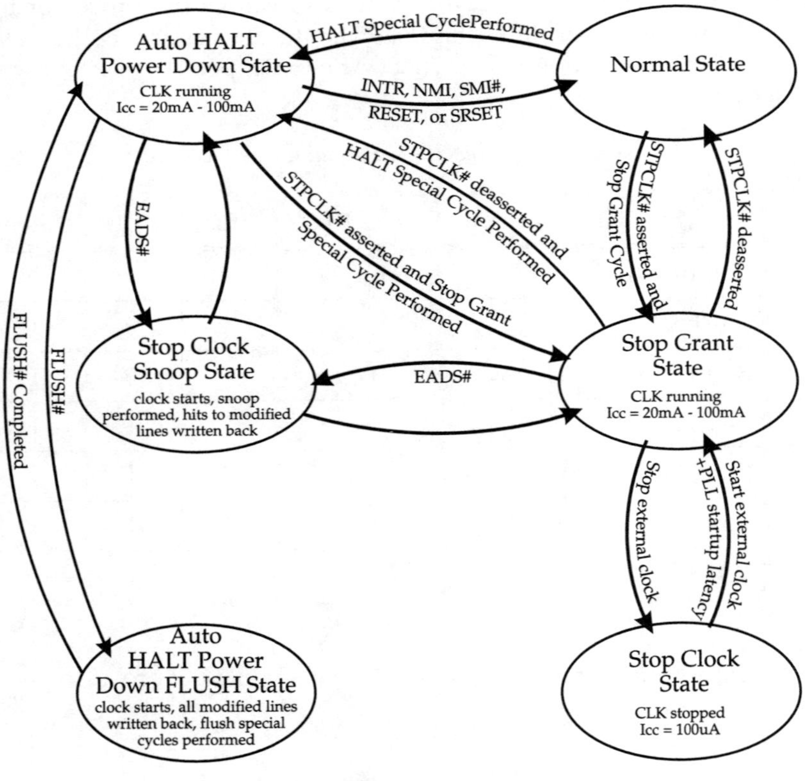

Figure 10-6. Stop Clock State Machine for Enhanced Bus Mode

These changes are due to the possibility that the cache will contain modified lines. The processor can perform external snoops while in the Stop Grant and Auto HALT Power Down states. If the processor detects a snoop hit to a modified line, must perform a write-back cycle to update external memory. The processor will not return from the Stop Clock Snoop state until the modified line has been written back.

Similarly, the processor monitors the FLUSH# pin while in the Auto HALT Power Down state. If the processor's FLUSH# pin is asserted the processor will write back all modified lines, invalid all cache entries and perform two flush acknowledge special cycles. Once the completed, the processor returns to the Auto HALT Power Down state.

Chapter 11

The Previous Chapter

The previous chapter discussed the features associated with the Enhanced Write Back 486DX2 and the differences between it and the standard 486DX2 processors. The chapter focused on new signals, the MESI model, special cycles, and cache line fill and snoop transactions.

This Chapter

This chapter overviews the 486DX4 processor and discusses the differences between the it and other 486 processors.

Primary Feature of the 486DX4 Processor

The 486DX4 processor contains a 486DX processor core and a full 64-bit data bus. The key features of the 486DX4 are:

- Input clock frequencies of 25MHz, 33MHz, or 50MHz
- Clock multiplying technology, providing three different core frequencies.
- 16KB internal cache
- 3.3vdc core logic with 5vdc tolerant I/O buffers

Clock Multiplier

The 486DX4 processor derives its core clock frequency by multiplying the external clock by a selectable multiplier ratio determined during RESET. The processor determines one of three clock multiplier ratios by sampling its clock multiplier input (CLKMUL). The multiplication options are:

- 2x — CLKMUL tied to Vss
- 2.5x — CLKMUL tied to BREQ
- 3x — CLKMUL tied to Vcc or no connection

Note that the CLKMUL pin has an internal pull-up resistor.

Table 11-1 lists the external and internal clock frequencies that are supported.

Table 11-1. External and Internal Clock Frequencies Supported by the 486DX4

Clock Multiplier	External Clock (MHz)	Internal Clock (MHz)
2	50	100
2.5	33	83
3	25 33	75 100

16KB Internal Cache

The 486DX4 processor's internal cache has the same basic organization as the 486DX processors, with the exception of the cache size. The 486DX4 has a 16KB cache, whereas all other 486 processors have an 8KB internal cache.

Table 11-2 compares the 486DX4 cache with that of the standard 486DX processor. Note that all 486 caches are unified caches (store both code and data), organized as four-way set associative, and maintain a write-through policy (except the Enhanced Write Back 486DX2 processor). The cache size difference impacts the number of entries in each cache directory and the number of lines in each of the four cache arrays.

Table 11-2. 486DX Cache Vs 486DX4 Cache

Cache Feature	486DX	486DX4
Cache Structure	unified	unified
Cache Size	8KB	16KB
Cache Associativity	4-way	4-way
Line Size	16 bytes	16 bytes
Line Replacement	Pseudo LRU	Pseudo LRU
Write Policy	write-through	write-through

The organization of the 486DX4 cache is illustrated in figure 11-1. Note that the cache size difference also changes the cache controllers view of the address. Since each of the four cache arrays is 4KB is size, each contain 256 lines (16 bytes each). Similarly, each directory contains 256 entries. The index portion of the address consists of 8 bits (A11:A4) and is used to identify the target entry that must be looked up in the directory. Each target entry is compared to the tag, or page portion of the address, both of which consist of address bits A31:A12.

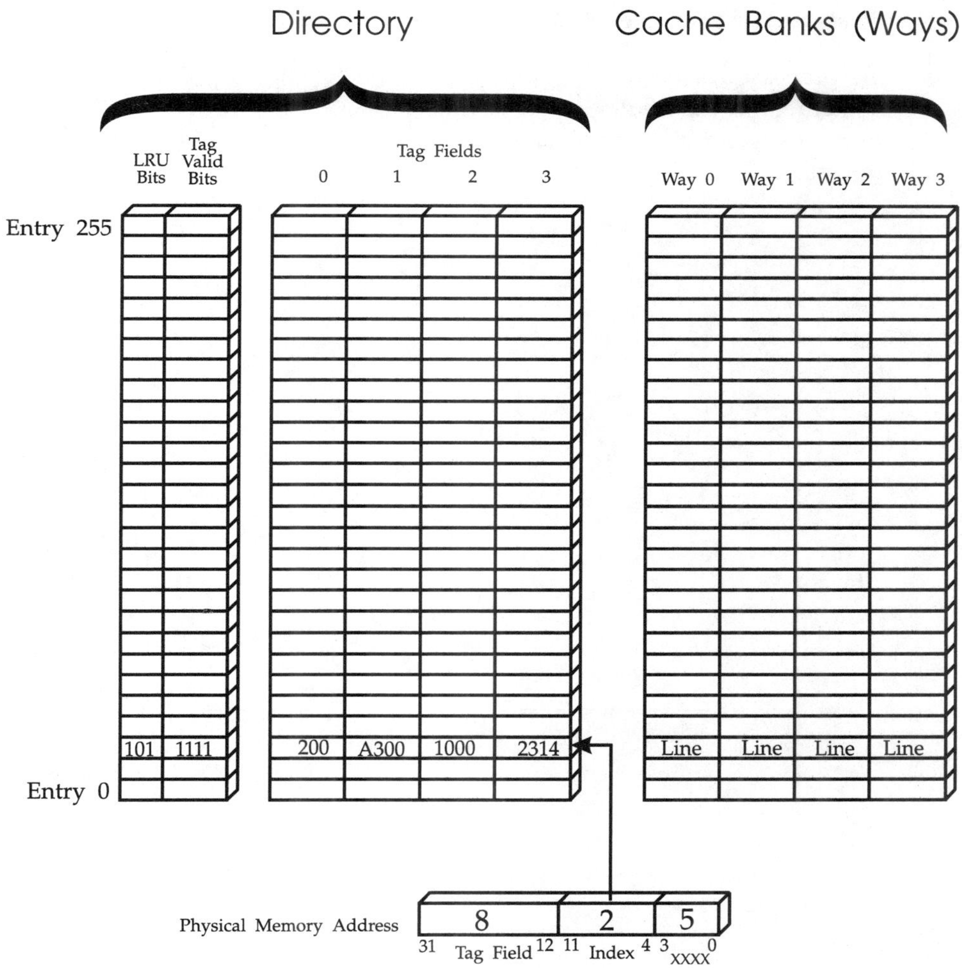

Figure 11-1. Organization of the 486DX4 Internal Cache

5vdc Tolerant Design

The 486DX4 processor operates only at 3.3vdc, however its input/output buffers have been designed to be 5vdc tolerant. One of the processor's Vcc pins (labeled Vcc5) is used to supply the buffers with a 5vdc reference. This pin should be connected to 3.3vdc if all inputs are from 3.3vdc logic.

The processor also has a VOLDET (voltage detect) output signal that is implemented on the PGA version of the 486DX4. This pin is intended to permit external system logic to distinguish between a 3.3vdc 486DX4 and 5vdc 486 processor.

Glossary

Glossary

4MB pages	The latest versions of the 486 processors permit page sizes of both 4KB and 4MB. The new 4MB page size improves the TLB hit rate.
Address Bus	The address bus used by the 486 processors consists of A31:A2 and BE3#:BE0#.
Address Status	An output from the 486 microprocessor that indicates that a valid address in on the bus.
Address Translation	The process of converting linear addresses to physical address when the processor is operating with paging enabled. Also used to describe the processor used by bus controllers to convert the native address driven by the processor into the forms recognizes by smaller devices (e.g. converting A31:A2 & BE3:BE0 to A23:A1 BHE#, & BLE#).
ADS#	See Address Status
AHOLD	See Address Hold
Address Hold	An input to the 486 microprocessor that notifies it that any address currently on its external address bus should be removed. This is done so that the 486 can snoop the address being passed to it from a secondary look-through cache controller.
Alignment Check bit	This bit is set in the flag register if an instruction causes a misaligned transfer to occur.
Auto-halt restart	An SMM feature allowing the processor to re-execute the HALT instruction upon exiting SMM, if the processor was in the halt state when the SMI# pin was asserted, or under software control the processor may be directed to execute the instruction following the halt instruction.

Boundary scan This is a test procedure that uses the 486 processor's test access port (TAP) interface to perform functional tests, typically used in manufacturing test.

BLAST# Burst Last. The Burst Last signal indicates that the next time BRDY# is returned, the burst cycle is complete. BLAST# is active for both burst and non-burst bus cycles.

BOFF# See Bus Backoff

BRDY# Burst Ready. When BRDY# is sampled active by the 486, it indicates to the microprocessor that the addressed memory subsystem has agreed to perform a burst transfer.

BREQ Bus Request. A 486 output signal that notifies external logic that the 486 needs ownership of the buses to run a bus cycle.

BS16# Bus Size 16. An input to the 486 telling it that the transfer is to or from a 16-bit device.

BS8# Bus Size 8. An input to the 486 telling it that the transfer is to or from an 8-bit device.

Burst bus cycle An 80486 bus cycle in which four doublewords can be transferred during a memory read operation. The first double word requires 2 PCLKs and the remaining three doubleword take 1 PCLK each for a total of five PCLKs per 16 byte burst.

Burst Last Burst Last (BLAST#). The Burst Last signal indicates that the next time BRDY# is returned, the burst cycle is complete. BLAST# is active for both burst and non-burst bus cycles.

Burst linefill sequence The sequence of doubleword address locations that the processor expects to be returned during a burst cache line fill. Also called toggle addressing.

Burst-mode transfer A 486 transfer that requires only five PCLKs to transfer sixteen bytes of information.

Bus Backoff Bus Backoff, BOFF#, is used by the write-back cache to force the 80486 to abort the bus cycle in progress. The BOFF# signal indicates that another bus master needs to complete a bus cycle in order for the microprocessor's current bus cycle to complete successfully.

Bus concurrency A single computer system having the ability to perform simultaneous operations over isolated buses.

Bus Cycle Definition Specifies the type of bus cycle being run. Memory read, memory write, I/O read, I/O write, Interrupt acknowledge, Halt or Shutdown.

Bus Cycle Restart Bus cycle restart. BOFF# causes the bus cycle to be aborted due to the possibility that the 486 is about to read stale data from memory. This can occur with a write-back cache implementation. When BOFF# is de-asserted by the write-back cache, the cycle is automatically restarted by the 486.

Bus snooping A process used by cache controllers to monitor memory address locations being accessed by other bus masters in a system. Snoop is done to detect memory transfers that might result in cache incoherency between the cache's contents and main memory.

Cache coherency This term refers to the state of a memory cache and system memory which ensures that the latest contents of a memory location is always supplied to a requester.

Cache controller A cache memory controller manages cache memory which stores copies of frequently accessed information read from DRAM memory.

Cache directory Memory inside of a cache controller that keeps track of information stored in cache memory. Sometimes called the tag RAM.

Cache Disable (CD) A bit within control register zero (CR0) in the 486 processors that, in conjunction with the NW bit, controls the operation of the internal caches.

Cache line A line is the smallest unit of data that a cache can keep track of. 4 double words in the 80486 internal cache.

Cache read hit The process in which the cache memory controller sees the microprocessor initiate a memory read bus cycle, checks to determine if it has a copy of the requested information in cache memory, and if a copy is present, immediately reads the information from the cache and sends it back to the microprocessor at zero wait-states.

Cache invalidation cycle When EADS# is asserted, the 486 snoops its external address bus to see if it has a copy of the address in its internal cache. If a snoop hit occurs the directory entry for that address will be invalidated.

Cache line fill In the 486 a cache line is sixteen bytes wide. When a request from memory results in a miss in the internal cache, it attempts to perform a cache line fill by reading 16 bytes of information to fill the cache line.

Cache memory Cache memory is a relatively small amount of high cost, fast access SRAM designed to improve access to system memory.

Cache not write-through (NW). A bit within control register zero (CR0) in the 486 processors that, in conjunction with the CD bit, controls the operation of the internal caches.

Cache read miss The process in which the cache memory controller sees the microprocessor initiate a memory read bus cycle, checks to determine if it has a copy of the requested information in cache memory, and finds no copy is present. The cache memory controller then passes the read bus cycle on to slow main memory.

Cache way The logical organization of cache memory that determines the number of ways (or places) a particular line of information can be stored in physical cache memory.

Cache write hit A write operation submitted to a cache subsystem, whose location resides within the memory cache, resulting in fast access.

Cache write miss A write operation submitted to a cache subsystem, whose address location is not found within cache memory.

Clean data Data contained within a memory cache that has not been modified. The cache location and system memory location are consistent.

Clock doubler Also called OverDrive. A 486 microprocessor that internally incorporates a clock-doubler feature that doubles the frequency of the clock signal supplied to the microprocessor by the off-chip crystal oscillator. All operations performed within the microprocessor are therefore executed at double the speed achievable by an 80486 that does not incorporate the clock-doubler capability.

CPUID instruction CPU Identification instruction. This new instruction permits the programmer to read the contents of the CPUID register to determine the processor class, type and revision.

CR4 Control Register four enables/disables new features, or extensions, implemented by the newer 486 processors.

D1 stage Stage one decode within the processors instruction pipeline where the opcodes are identified and the instruction pairing test is performed.

D2 stage Stage two decode within the processors instruction pipeline where addresses are formed when memory operands are accessed.

Data bus steering The process of transferring bytes of data between data paths to ensure information gets to the intended destination. This is sometimes required when data is transferred between devices of differing sizes. The 486 processors contain no data bus steering logic, therefore it must be implemented in external logic.

D/C# One of the 486 bus cycle definition line outputs that defines whether the bus cycle being run is an access to data or code within memory.

Debug registers Six programmer-accessible debug registers provide on-chip support for debugging and are present in both the 80386 and 80486. Debug registers DR0 through DR3 specify the four linear breakpoint addresses. The Breakpoint Control Register, DR7, is used to set the breakpoints, define them as data or code breakpoints, and whether to break on an attempted read or write. The Breakpoint Status Register, DR6, reflects the current state of the breakpoints.

Dirty bit A bit in a in the page directory entries that when set, indicates that the operating system should ensure that the page is written back to disk to maintain coherency between disk and main memory.

Dirty line A line in cache memory that has been updated by the microprocessor by not in main memory. The 80486 executes a special bus cycle to command the external cache to write all dirty lines back to main memory and flush its contents (if it's a write-back cache).

External address status When EADS# is asserted, the 486 snoops its external address bus to see if it has a copy of the address in its internal cache. If a snoop hit occurs the directory entry for that address will be invalidated.

EFLAGS register The Extended Flag register in the 386 and 486.

Exclusive state A MESI state indicating that no other cache controllers possess a copy of this cache line, therefore it is owned exclusively by this cache.

External cache A cache located physically outside of the microprocessor. Usually refers to a secondary cache that is multiple times larger than the first level cache inside the processor.

First level cache A cache integrated into the processor, making it the first cache to be accessed during a memory read or write operation.

Floating-Point Unit The unit inside the 486 that executes floating-point instructions. It is functionally equivalent to the 80387 Numeric Coprocessor.

FLUSH# An input to the 486 microprocessor that when active, causes all of the internal cache controller's Tag Valid bits to be cleared. If held active this has the effect of disabling the cache. FLUSH# cause modified lines to be written back to memory prior to the cache being flushed in the Write Back Enhanced 486DX2 processor.

Flush acknowledge special cycle This special cycle is run by the Write Back Enhanced 486DX2 processor in response to the FLUSH# pin having been asserted. This causes the processor to write-back all modified lines to memory, invalidate all cache entries and perform two flush acknowledge special cycle to notify external logic that the operation has completed.

Four-way set associative cache A cache organization that provides four cache memory banks (ways) in which information can be stored.

Hold acknowledge A microprocessor output that notifies the request device that the microprocessor has given up ownership of the buses.

HLDA See Hold Acknowledge.

HOLD See Hold Request.

Hold request A microprocessor input that is used by bus masters to gain ownership of the buses.

IDTR See Interrupt Descriptor Table Register

Interrupt descriptor table register A register in protected mode processors that keeps the starting address in main memory where the interrupt descriptor table resides.

IGNNE# Ignore Numeric Error. A 486 Input signal used when in DOS compatible mode to direct the internal floating-point unit to continue processing after an error condition has been encountered.

Inquire cycles A snoop transaction performed by the Write Back Enhanced 486DX2 processor as directed by external logic, resulting from a bus master read. The snoop results are reported via the HITM# signal. The cache line is not invalidated as a result of a snoop hit.

Interleaved memory A DRAM memory architecture in which memory banks are paired and connected such that sequential bank addresses result in alternating access to each bank. This architecture reduces the effect of precharge delay which slows access to DRAM memory.

Interrupt acknowledge A signal sent to the interrupt controller to indicate that its request is being acknowledged.

Interrupt descriptor An entry within the interrupt descriptor table that specifies the location in memory of an interrupt service routine.

Interrupt descriptor table register A register in protected mode processors that identify where the interrupt descriptor table resides in memory.

Interrupt request An input to the microprocessor that notifies it that an interrupt driven I/O needs servicing.

Interrupted burst In some cases, a memory subsystem may not be able to respond with the four requested doublewords in the order required while performing a burst cache line fill. More time may be required between the reading of some or all of the doublewords in which case the burst bus cycle will be interrupted.

INTR See Interrupt Request

INVD Invalidate cache instruction. A 486 instruction that causes an external cache to invalidate its contents.

INVLPG The INVLPG instruction invalidates a single entry in the Translation Lookaside Buffer (TLB). The programmer specifies a memory location using virtual (paging) addressing. If the specified address has a corresponding entry in the TLB, it will be marked invalid.

I/O instruction restart The SMM feature that permits the processor to re-execute an I/O instruction (the instruction that accessed a device that was powered down, causing entry to SMM) upon returning from SMM.

KEN# Cache Enable. Tell the microprocessor that the location being accessed is a cacheable location.

LDTR Local Descriptor Table Register. Found in a protected mode processors. Specifies the location in memory of the local descriptor table for a given application.

Line A line is the smallest unit of information that a cache controller can track. 4 double words (16bytes) in the 80486 internal cache.

Linear address The address output from the segmentation unit when paging is enabled.

LOCK# The processor asserts LOCK# when executing instructions prefaced by the LOCK prefix or during certain other multiple bus cycles when the processor does not want the buses stolen between bus cycles.

Look-Aside Cache A cache memory design in which the cache controller sets in parallel with main system memory. When memory is addressed both the cache controller and system memory are addressed. Compare Look-through Cache.

Look-through cache A cache memory design in which memory request go first to the cache controller which looks through its cache memory to determine if this request is a hit or miss. If the information is not in cache then the bus cycle is broadcast on to main memory.

LRU algorithm Least Recently Used Algorithm. Used in cache memory designs to determine which cache entry is to be overwritten by newer data. Conforms to the principle of temporal locality.

M/IO# Memory or I/O#. The signal output from the microprocessor that informs external logic whether the address on the bus is for memory or I/O devices.

MESI model A cache coherency model in which a cache line may be stored in any one of four states: Modified, Exclusive, Shared and Invalid. See each state for definitions.

Microcode control ROM The ROM inside x86 processors that contains the processor commands necessary to execute complex instructions.

Misaligned access In a 486, a four byte transfer that crosses an even doubleword boundary causing the 486 to run two bus cycles to complete the transfer.

Modified line A cache line that has been updated due to a write hit in the cache. Also known as a dirty line.

NE Mask Numeric Error bit. Determines the manner in which the 486 handles the numeric error -- standard or DOS compatible mode.

NMI Non-maskable Interrupt. Used to report serious error conditions to the microprocessor.

Non-cacheable access A memory read operation from a location that is specified not to be cached.

NCA logic Monitors Addresses from the microprocessor and specifies which address locations should not be cached.

OverDrive processor Upgrade processor that incorporate a clock multiplier feature that internally increases the frequency of the clock signal supplied to the microprocessor core by the off-chip crystal oscillator. All operations performed within the microprocessor are therefore executed at higher speeds than that achievable by the original processor.

Page cache disable A bit in the page table entries that specifies whether a page of memory is to be considered cacheable or non-cacheable by the 486.

Page directory A data structure set up by the operating system that defines the location of Page Tables. The page directory and page tables are needed to translate linear to physical addresses when paging is enabled.

Page size extension The extension added to newer 486 processors that allows 4MB pages to be implemented.

Page fault A processor exception that occurs during paging when the desired page isn't currently present in main memory.

Page fault handler The handler routine called when a page fault occurs.

Page present bit A bit in the directory entry that specifies if the 4KB page in present in memory or not.

Page table An area of main memory that contains 1024 entries that point to the starting address of a 1024 individual pages. Used when the 486 is in page address mode.

Page write-through bit A bit in the page table entries that specifies that locations from page of memory are to be written through to main memory when a write-back cache is implemented as a secondary cache.

Paging, virtual The 80386/80486 paging system that provides an indexing system to keep track of the location and status of up to 1,048,576 4KB pages (4GB) of program and/or data that "belongs" to a task (applications program). At a given moment in time, a page of program and/or data can be in memory or on disk.

Parity A reliability measure used to notify the system that information read from memory is not the same as the information initially written.

PCD See Page Cache Disable.

PCHK# The 80486 output that is asserted if a parity error is detected on a read operation.

PCLK cycles Processor Clock. The clock used by the processor to run external bus cycles.

Performance socket A system that uses the "performance" socket pinout can be upgraded to a 80486SX OverDrive processor.

PLOCK# See Pseudo-Lock.

Prefetcher Performs speculative in-line memory reads, to obtain the next instructions to be executed. Operates on the assumption that the instruction stream resides in sequentially in memory.

Pseudo-Lock This 486 output is active during certain 486 transfers that require multiple bus cycles to perform, such as a burst bus cycle.

PWT See Page write-through.

Read hit See Cache read hit

Read miss See Cache read miss

RSM instruction Return from System Management Mode instruction. This instruction is the last instruction executed by the SMM handler. When executed, the processor returns to normal program execution.

Write-through policy A type of write policy in which the cache controller updates main system memory immediately

Segment descriptor An entry within the segment descriptor table in main memory used in protected mode address generation to specify the starting address of a segment of extended memory.

Shutdown special cycle A special cycle performed by the 486 processor when it encounters a triple fault condition.

Snoop A technique used by cache memory controllers to monitor the system buses to detect an access to main memory that might cause a cache consistency problem.

SMI handler The system management interrupt service routine. This routine is responsible for determining the cause of the SMI and performing the requisite tasks. Upon completion, it executes the RSM instruction.

SMI The system management interrupt causes the processor to enter the SMM mode of operation.

SMM System Management Mode. This operational mode permits tasks such as power management relatively easy to implement, since the address space that is accessed to perform such tasks is transparent to the operating system and application programs.

SMM base address The base address at which the SMRAM resides within the 1MB of real address space.

SMM revision identifier A register value that reflects the SMM extensions supported by a particular processor.

SMM state save map The processor's current state (context) is mapped to SMRAM before entering SMM, permitting the return to the interrupted program. When the RSM instruction executes the state save map is restored to the processor and it continues program execution at the point of interruption.

SMRAM System Management RAM is used to implement the SMI handler and store the processor's state.

Snarf A cache memory implementation that snoops memory write transfers and automatically updates, rather than invalidating, the cache entries that hit the cache.

Special cycles Transaction broadcast on the 486 processor's local bus to indicate one of the following conditions: halt, shutdown, flush (INVD or WBINVD instruction executed), write-back (WBINVD instruction executed), flush acknowledge (FLUSH# pin asserted, Write Back Enhanced processor only) or the stop grant message (in response to STPCLK# being asserted).

Stale data In a cache memory system, data in cache or in main memory that has not been updated to reflect a change in the other copy.

Stop grant state The processor enters the stop grant state to notify external logic that it has stopped its internal clock in response to the STPCLK# signal being asserted.

Tag Valid bit A bit contained in a cache directory entry that specifies if the associated cache location contains valid data.

TAP The Test Access Port is a five signal serial interface that supports boundary scan testing.

TLB See Translation Look-aside Buffer.

Translation look-aside buffer The TLB is a four-way set associative 32-entry Page Table cache. It automatically keeps the most-recently used Page Table entries in the processor when the processor is in paging address mode.

W/R# Write or read. Used by the microprocessor to either specify whether the current bus cycle is a write or read operation.

WBINVD instruction Write Back and Invalidate instruction. Used by the 486 to direct an external write-back cache to write all dirty lines back to main memory and flush its contents (if it's a write-back cache).

Write-back policy A cache coherency policy that updates its cache on memory write operations, but does not write the data on through to external memory. Such caches implement modified, or dirty bits to track which locations contain the latest information (and which memory location contain stale data). The write-back policy requires that cache controllers snoop both memory reads and writes, and either back the bus master off to prevent access to a location containing stale data, or employ snarfing to ensure other bus masters always obtain the latest data.

Write-back special cycle A special cycle performed by the 486 processor when a WBINVD instruction is executed. The 486 Write Back Enhanced processor performs the write-back special cycle after it has written all modified cache lines back to memory. It then performs a flush special cycle.

Write buffers Four buffers in the Bus Unit that allow it to buffer up to four write bus cycles from the processor, permitting these write operations to complete execution instantly.

Write hit The process in which the cache memory controller sees the microprocessor initiate a memory write bus cycle, checks to determine if it has a copy of the requested information in cache memory, and if a copy is present, immediately updates the information in cache and sends ready to the processor which ends the bus cycle in zero wait-states.

Write miss The process in which the cache memory controller sees the microprocessor initiate a memory write bus cycle, checks to determine if it has a copy of the requested information in cache memory, and finds no copy is present. The cache memory controller then passes the write bus cycle on to slow main memory.

Write-back cache A type of write policy in which the cache controller only updates main system memory when necessary.

Write-through cache A cache that adheres to the write-through policy, in which the cache controller updates main system memory immediately on any write to cache

Write-through policy A policy, in which the cache controller updates main system memory immediately on any write to cache. On write hits this ensures that the memory location updated in cache is also updated in main memory.

Index

Index

T

U

V

W

X